# The OM Factor®

Go within and find your OM factor.

Best,

# The OM Factor®

## A WOMAN'S SPIRITUAL GUIDE TO LEADERSHIP

Alka Dhillon

*7 Essential Tools and 7 Key Traits to Cultivate for Your Success and Well-Being*

SelectBooks, Inc.
*New York*

This edition published by SelectBooks, Inc.
For information address SelectBooks, Inc., New York, New York.

First Edition

ISBN 978-1-59079-299-5

*Cataloging-in-Publication Data*
Dhillon, Alka.
The OM factor : a woman's spiritual guide to leadership / Alka Dhillon. -- First edition.
pages cm
"7 essential tools and 7 key traits to cultivate for your success and well-being."
Summary: "Author introduces The OM Factor ®, the traits that admirable leaders, often women, nurture to be in tune with their body, mind, and spirit. She describes seven tools, including Eastern spiritual practices of meditation and yoga, and seven traits of The OM Factor that women can cultivate to achieve success. Contains yoga poses, mantras, affirmations, and poetry"-- Provided by publisher.
ISBN 978-1-59079-299-5 (pbk. : alk. paper)
1. Leadership in women. I. Title.
HQ1233.D488 2015
303.3'4082--dc23

2014037708

Book design by Janice Benight

Manufactured in the United States of America
10 9 8 7 6 5 4 3 2 1

*This book is dedicated to my late father,*

*Madan Lal Sethi*

*Daddy, thank you for the gift of your*

*Finite amount of time on this earth making an*

*Infinite impact on my life.*

*I love you.*

# CONTENTS

# Part I

# UNDERSTANDING THE OM FACTOR

# MY STORY

## Youthful Entrepreneurism and a Family Tragedy

I WAS BITTEN BY THE ENTREPRENEURIAL bug at around age seven. As a first generation Indian-American I have been blessed to have the opportunity to truly carve my destiny in this beautiful country of ours. When I was a child, my father would bring me during the summer to the restaurant he owned to "learn" about the restaurant business. To me it felt like I was just being a dishwasher and floor mopper, and—if I was lucky—I was allowed to count the money in the register. My father would say, "In order to be successful running any type of business you must know how to do every aspect of the operation yourself. In the event the person tasked with that aspect is not around, the ship keeps sailing."

*Okay, I get it. But why so much time washing dishes?* I thought I had that part down a lot sooner than he did, I guess. In time, what I realized was that in order to be truly good at something you must practice. It should become second nature to you. I also realized that everything he asked me to do has helped me run my company successfully to this day.

I was twenty-four years old when my father passed away suddenly from a heart attack. One minute I was a young, carefree girl working in DC, and the next minute I was transformed into a distressed, responsible woman. As the eldest child with my two sisters aged twenty-one and seventeen, I was the one who had to step up and be a support beam for the family, both financially and emotionally. In three months, both of my younger sisters would be graduating. One would be graduating from her university and the other would be graduating from high school and going on to college. My mother was and is one of the strongest women I have had the privilege of knowing. She never let us see her sorrow, which we knew from losing the love of her life so suddenly after twenty-six years of marriage, was to depths that most people could not imagine.

Since my father had been the primary earner in the family, it was clear to me that it was my responsibility to make sure that my youngest sister continue with her education as well as to ensure that my family continue to be provided for in the way my father had done for our entire lives.

I immediately left my apartment in the city and moved back into my parents' home in order for us to try to navigate through our individual and collective pain together. I found myself focusing on trying to make as much money as possible so that I could not only provide for my family, but have enough to take them on vacations for a change of scenery and to do things together where the pain could be lessened by a perceived change in our circumstance, even though we were only physically changing locations. With the help of the universe and some good luck we were fine financially.

Emotionally, it was an entirely other story. All of us tried to deal with the pain in our own ways—which was mainly to not deal with it and just move forward through life. I, in particular, tried to block it out of my mind as much as possible in order to not lose my focus and my primary purpose: to support my family. This was the biggest mistake that I made.

I did not nourish my physical and emotional body. I did not eat the proper food or eat regularly. Nor did I allow myself to talk about my loss and pain to someone who could help me process what had happened and begin the healing process.

I began to experience chest pain as well as non-specific muscle and joint pain. I had palpitations and trouble breathing. One day I tried to get out of bed and my legs wouldn't move. I made several trips to the emergency room and no one could figure out what was wrong with me. One day, I looked at myself in the mirror and I could not even recognize myself. It was not only that I couldn't recognize myself physically; I honestly didn't know who that woman was in the mirror. It is those times when you feel you are at your lowest point and there is no way out or up, that the universe sends you a message. How or when or what form that message comes in can be elusive, but a shift happens.

***It is those times when you feel you are at your lowest point and there is no way out or up, that the universe sends you a message. How or when or what form that message comes in can be elusive, but a shift happens.***

The woman in the mirror looked back at me with a message in her eyes saying, "Go down a different path. You need to wake up and get up." That day, I decided to enroll in a yoga class and learn meditation. I began to take yoga a few times a week, and those classes would have meditation at the beginning and end of the class. After a month, I not only did not set foot into an emergency room, but I experienced a change in the way I saw and perceived my surroundings.

Learning meditation enabled me to go beyond my physical body and physical experiences and open myself up to perceiving things through a different lens. Honestly, nothing had changed in my circumstances. My father was still dead. The grief was still horrific. However, instead of having trouble walking at times or breathing, I was able to function and breathe through the grief. I felt an inner sense of strength which enabled me to move forward on my journey through life and navigate through what was to come next in my path.

## The Meaning of *the OM Factor*

Often chanted three times at the start and finish of a yoga session, "OM" is a very simple chant with a complex meaning. When chanted, the sound of the word OM is actually pronounced in three syllables as if spelled with the letters a, u, and m. OM is the whole universe encapsulated in a single sound and represents the union of mind, body, and spirit.

When I was thinking about the intrinsic qualities of someone who flows through life successfully and makes it seem effortless, I noticed that these people are really in tune with all aspects of themselves: their body, mind, and spirit. They look healthy and have a glow about them. They are very sharp and quick to respond. They are also extremely aware of themselves and their actions. I then realized that these people have that special something that enabled their success. I coined it *The OM Factor*.

Today, seventeen years later, I have in common with millions of other women the title of mother, CEO, sister, daughter, and wife. This art of balancing harmoniously all these roles and relationships, being holistic in our approach to our well-being, as well as being successful at whatever we do in the workplace and at home during most of our waking hours, is the OM Factor.

But one thing I have realized is that what women tend not to share as a group is bringing the many aspects of our spirituality into our workplace—whether that work is in the office, home, or wherever we spend the majority of our time working.

The presence of spirituality in the business world or in any institution is clearly important. I am not, of course, talking here about following a dogma of organized religion. I am referring to true spirituality—having a path that guides and allows a person to discover the essence of his or her being by looking within, as demonstrated by successful women who have the OM Factor.

It is my intention that what will unfold over the course of reading this book is that people will acquire a road map to discover not only what their own personal OM Factor is, but how to increase it in themselves and others around them. I have taken very common feelings that arise in our daily lives and provided practical and tangible ways in which to deal with them more spiritually, for people ultimately to become much more successful and happy.

I have provided **actual** tools in part two that you can immediately use to handle these scenarios acutely and "in the moment." In part three I demonstrate how to repair the root of the reason the situation became untenable and anxiety provoking in the first place by developing the spiritual traits that are key to being able to handle life's curveballs, as well as reducing the frequency of them appearing in your life.

You cannot heal a deep wound immediately. First, you need to deal with stopping the bleeding, and then you can address healing it at a deeper level and ideally preventing it from happening again in the future. If it does occur in the future you will know how to handle healing the wound in a manner that is not haphazard and chaotic, but rather holistic and tranquil.

Those individuals who have the OM Factor (and a high one at that) are able to deal with challenging situations as they arise. They have learned to not **react** involuntarily to difficult situations but to intentionally **respond** to them, as I define and describe the differences between these two kinds of behavior in the following pages. These people flow. They are able to do this by constantly being very aware of their deep and direct connection to their source—their spirit. It is effortless for them because they are aware of who they are at the core, truly no different from anyone or anything around them. They are one with the universe. Spirit has no color, no shape or size. Spirit is universal. It is like air.

We all breathe the same air; however, some of us breathe in quickly and some more slowly. It is the same with spirit. We all have it, but some of us are more aware and connected to it than others. The good news is, like breathing, it takes a millisecond to change your experience . . . fast or slow, awake or asleep. It is all in your control and all your choice: What is your OM Factor and what would you like it to be?

# OM

*I will give you the Word that*
*all the scriptures glorify,*
*all spiritual disciplines express,*
*to attain which aspirants lead a life*
*of sense-restraint and self-naughting*
*It is OM.*

*This symbol of the Godhead is the highest.*
*Realizing it one finds complete*
*fulfillment of all one's longings.*
*It is of the greatest support to all seekers.*

*Those in whose hearts OM*
*Reverberates unceasingly*
*are indeed blessed*
*and deeply loved*
*as one who is the Self.*

—Katha Upanishad

# NURTURING YOUR OM FACTOR

All persons who have a high OM Factor do some form of physical yoga and meditation or have an affirmation-based dialogue with themselves. There is no doubt in their minds that they are divinely guided and that every situation has shown up in their life for a reason, and there is a lesson in it. They always look within for answers by going into silence. Because this is so important, I am going to define and demystify the concepts of meditation, mantras, and affirmations so that you can have a strong spiritual foundation when reading the rest of the book.

You have infinite divine power within yourself, which is something that many people do not believe and therefore are always looking elsewhere for answers. As the poet Kabir profoundly expressed:

*The fish in the water*
*is racked by thirst:*
*I hear about it*
*and burst out laughing.*
*What you are looking for*
*is right at home*
*and yet you roam from forest to forest,*
*full of gloom . . .*

—Kabir

Anyone, at any age, can practice these techniques of meditation and the reciting of mantras and/or affirmations, and this will work for you every time. It is the one sure thing—the one sure bet in life. You know why being a spiritual person works? It works because you are accessing your own inner light and source to fuel your own personal journey through life.

## What Is Meditation and How Do You Do It?

> Meditation, by definition, is *a practice of concentrated focus upon a sound, object, visualization, the breath, movement, or attention itself in order to increase awareness of the present moment, reduce stress, promote relaxation, and enhance personal and spiritual growth.*

The sheer concept or idea of practicing meditation is anxiety provoking for many, as it seems like this is an unattainable and insurmountable task akin to climbing Mount Kilimanjaro in the dead of winter. Many have done it, but we feel they must be superhuman or have trained tirelessly every day to prepare for such a feat. I would like to lift the veil here. The practice of meditation is just simply a technique for entering a state of being by observing your breath in the present moment. Nothing more and nothing less. It's not sexy, but the result is provocative and powerful.

Whatever time you have to practice this will be a priceless gift to yourself. Whether you meditate two minutes or one hour is really not important. Those two minutes will eventually turn into several minutes, because it is so addictive. This is because your body and mind are united and become one during meditation. It's like the perfect tango—elegant yet bold at the same time. Who doesn't like the tango and wouldn't like to do it whenever they got the chance if they performed it beautifully? Whenever you have the opportunity, preferably in the morning before starting your daily routine, take a few minutes to sit in silence and simply observe your breath.

Find a place to practice meditation where you feel comfortable. Ideally, it's somewhere in your home or office where you can create a sacred space for yourself. "Sacred space" simply means a space that you have set aside as a special spot for this nourishment of your being. If you are a visual person you can create a small altar and have aesthetically pleasing pillows, pictures, and candles in your space. None of these items are necessary; however, sometimes they do provide the ambiance that some visually inclined people require to attune themselves to the practice.

For those who are not stimulated visually by these objects, all you need is the space required for your body to be seated. Sit easily and comfortably, with your spine straight, either on the floor with your legs crossed or in a chair with your feet flat on the floor. Then simply **observe your breath**. Observe the inhalation and exhalation of your breath without trying to control it. This is the place where you can truly let go and just be. You have nowhere to be but in this space at this moment, and nothing is more important than this moment. Because we live in the physical world of deadlines and schedules, you can set a timer on your phone or clock for however many minutes you would like to start with.

A very important suggestion I have regarding meditation is to not judge whether you are doing it right. There is no right or wrong, no winning or losing—*that* is the big breaking news. I cannot tell you how many people have said to me "I cannot meditate because I have thoughts." Do not judge yourself negatively if you are having "thoughts." If you do, congratulations; you are a living, breathing human being and you exist. Everyone has thoughts.

However, as you begin to meditate for a longer period of time, you will observe that there is a space between Thought A and Thought B. It is in that space where the inner silence and stillness you feel exists. That is where your true essence resides. That is where the magic really happens.

What people refer to as enlightenment is just an infinitely longer experience of that space between thought A and thought B. This is the paradise that we are all looking to feel and experience: true bliss.

As you begin to meditate for a longer period of time, you will observe that there is a space between thought A and thought B. It is in that space where the inner silence and stillness you feel exists. That is where your true essence resides. That is where the magic really happens.

***As you begin to meditate for a longer period of time, you will observe that there is a space between thought A and thought B. It is in that space where the inner silence and stillness you feel exists. That is where your true essence resides. That is where the magic really happens.***

After your individually allotted time has passed and the timer has gone off, just sit still and quietly for about a minute or so to recalibrate before you resume any tasks and go about your day.

Now that the mystery and anxiety about practicing meditation has been lifted, I hope you will realize that everyone has time to practice this. Making meditation a priority will truly help heal any deep wounds, challenges, or emotional turbulence that you may be experiencing. Block it off on your calendar as you would any meeting or any appointment. It is one meeting that will always render profitable results.

## What Are Mantras and Affirmations?

A *mantra,* by definition, is *a sacred utterance (syllable, word, or verse), believed to possess spiritual power.*

Mantras may be spoken aloud or uttered in thought, and they may be either repeated or sounded only once. Most have no apparent verbal meaning, but they are thought to have profound significance and to serve as distillations of spiritual wisdom. Repetitions of a mantra can lead the participant to a higher level of spiritual awareness. Widely used mantras include "OM" in Hinduism and "OM MANI PADME HUM" in Tibetan Buddhism.

Affirmations are positive statements or messages that can be repeated to one's self silently or aloud to create an attitude of self-empowerment. A person can choose to use them before, during, or after meditation. Affirmations that are heard or repeated often can have a profound and pronounced effect on the user. Positive high-impact phrases can actually change your life for the better and have a counter-effect to the negative messages, feelings, or emotions that you may be experiencing.

There are many feelings and emotions that we experience in life when we perceive we are in a stressful situation or when dealing with people that appear to be challenging. Quietly or silently repeating a mantra or affirmation during these times can immediately diffuse the situation and enable you to "respond" rather than to simply "react." This is the key to handling a situation successfully.

I feel "reacting" to a situation is more of an instinctive and unconscious fight or flight action, utilizing little or no thought, whereas "responding" to a situation means that you have developed a method to process the challenge and consciously and thoughtfully deal with it in a more solution-oriented manner.

Chances are that by responding to the situation instead of reacting, you realize that it is no longer a challenge, but rather one that has a positive solution for everyone involved. This is the place you want to evolve to. Quietly or silently repeating the mantra or affirmation during these times can immediately diffuse the situation and enable you to respond rather than react.

In the chapters on the tools that follow, I will give an affirmation in English to use as well as an ancient mantra in Sanskrit that can also be used during these acute situations. It does not matter which one you choose to use; what matters is that you repeat it and that its vibrations resonate with you. These mantras and affirmations are very powerful since the act of repeating any sound produces a physical vibration. This vibration corresponds to a spiritual energy frequency and a state of consciousness.

***Quietly or silently repeating the mantra or affirmation during these times can immediately diffuse the situation and enable you to respond rather than react.***

When practiced repeatedly, a mantra elicits a subtle change in the person, and the person vibrates in tune with the energy and spiritual state contained in the mantra. This stills any and all other vibrations, and the mind becomes quiet and calm. The mind then begins to work in a different way. You are effectively replacing the white noise of your thoughts and external ambient noise with this spiritual and powerful vibration. If you combine this vibration of the mantra with a mental intention, it then provides a direct line to fulfill all your desires and will lead you toward what the Buddhists call Nirvana or Enlightenment.

Alternatively, you can make up your own mantras/affirmations. As you repeat the affirmation or mantra throughout the waking hours of your daily life, you will notice a calming down of your nervous system as the sounds wash over your body. You will also notice that the situation or challenge that was eliciting the response has probably changed as well. As Max Planck, the German physicist who discovered quantum physics, astutely observed, "When you change the way you look at things, the things you look at change."

## Implementing These Instruments in Daily Life

When you awaken every morning, try to sit in silence, not only to set the tone and intention of the day, but to also repair any damage that has been done from negative thoughts, the environment, or the stresses and pressures of your daily life. Remember, it does not matter how long you sit. Ideally, if you can work up to twenty minutes or longer this is great. If not, even two minutes makes a profound difference. What matters is consistency.

If you are able, try to also sit in silence in the evening or just before you retire if your schedule does not permit time for this earlier in the day. During this time you also may choose to recite a mantra, an affirmation, or simply observe your breath. This is a personal choice.

All the ways described are very powerful and you must find the ones that work for you. You may choose to do different things on different days. You may only have time in the morning or only time in the evening. Again, what is most important is not to worry about how much time you have for this, but to make whatever time you can for it every day. Consistency is what is key to having success. I cannot stress that enough.

If you decide to do a mantra/affirmation-based meditation you can silently repeat the mantra or affirmation as you inhale and exhale without worrying about timing it with the breaths you take. It is the vibration that is important and the intention that has the power.

If you choose, you may also use a *mala* (a Hindu or Buddhist rosary) with 108 beads to keep count of the repetitions. This way your eyes can be closed and you can slowly allow your thumb to advance each bead. You will not have to be preoccupied with how many times you have repeated the mantra or affirmation.

Most malas will have one big bead that connects the mala together and is believed to harness the power of all of the recitations of the mantra. This is called a meru bead. This bead should not be crossed over. You start at the first bead below the meru bead and continue until you reach the last bead before the meru bead. If you feel ambitious and want to do it again in one sitting, then upon reaching the last bead, reverse the direction and repeat it another 108 times so as not to cross the meru bead.

I know many of you are thinking, "What will happen if I accidently 'cross over' the meru bead. Will everything I have done be for nothing?" Nothing catastrophic will happen if you accidently cross over the meru bead. I am simply giving you the manner in which it is usually taught and the way I practice it. Remember, everything in this universe resides on the premise of intention. If your intention is pure and in line with the vibration of the universe, then it will always be manifested no matter what you do technically.

According to ancient scriptures, the heart chakra is where the soul and self resides. From this chakra, 108 *nadis*—or channels—extend out to all parts of our subtle body. This is why the number 108 is so significant. When we chant the mantra or affirmation

108 times it allows the essence, energy, and vibration of the mantra to enter all of the nadis, and it reaches all parts of the subtle body.

When doing your mantra/affirmation-based meditation in the morning or evening there are two things to keep in mind:

> **First, if it is a mantra that you choose to use for meditation, make sure it is something that really resonates with you and you feel drawn to it.**

Even the simple mantra of "I AM" is extremely powerful, as this is what is believed in many traditions to be the sound and vibration of God. Mantras allow us to make a more direct connection with the divine within ourselves as we are attuning to the vibration of the sacred sounds. If it is an affirmation that you choose to use, make sure that it is an "I am" statement referring to whatever it is that you would like to manifest, such as "I am healthy." "I am creative." "I am in a divine relationship." "I am grateful."

> **Second, you must be able to imagine or picture what it is that you are trying to manifest or believe.**

If you are unable to conjure up the image and believe that image to be your reality, then the universe will not be able to give you that which you cannot perceive. They are simply words. Remember, words have no meaning until and unless we attach an image to them.

If there is one thing that you can consciously commit to that will guarantee to improve your experience of life and improve the outcome of your interactions and activities, it is "to be present by truly experiencing and participating in the present moment." One very easy way to do that is to take a split second and simply inhale and exhale. The mere act of consciously taking in a breath and exhaling that breath brings you into your body and into the present moment. This is a tool that I use daily and it works every time.

This is the long-term maintenance that is required to bring yourself to a state of equilibrium, and just as the gap between the thoughts becomes larger and larger when you meditate, you will also notice the gap between feelings of being overwhelmed getting wider as well. This is the gift.

## The Practice of Yoga

When you train both your mental and physical aspects of your body, you are connecting your mind and body and enabling them to work in harmony. Yoga is a great way to train the physical aspect of your body. Yoga, by definition, is "*yoking*" or uniting the mind and body through a series of physical *asanas* or postures. The practice of Yoga is so powerful because you are essentially getting a "two for one" while training physically. I have included a yoga pose or yogic breathing exercise after each key trait in part III of the book to help connect your mental practice with a physical one. When you do this, it solidifies your efforts by making an imprint of the mental message of the key trait you are trying to cultivate that particular day within your physical body.

The poses I have suggested can be done anywhere according to your physical abilities. I have included poses that almost anyone can do without much physical strain. In fact, they feel great! Please do only what feels comfortable to you. Remember, this is not a race or a competition. This is a journey that you are on where you are your own companion and there is no fixed destination.

Please also make sure to check with your physician if you have any preexisting conditions that may preclude you from doing the poses. This is truly a spiritual practice that will increase your personal OM Factor and enable you to manifest any intention that you choose to set and also allow you to overcome any preexisting perceived turbulence or challenge in your life.

# IN THE STILL MIND

*When meditation is mastered,*
*The mind is unwavering like the*
*Flame of a lamp in a windless place.*
*In the still mind,*
*In the depths of meditation,*
*The Self reveals itself.*
*Beholding the Self*
*By means of the Self,*
*An aspirant knows the*
*Joy and peace of complete fulfillment.*
*Having attained that*
*Abiding joy beyond the senses,*
*Revealed in the stilled mind,*
*He never swerves from the eternal truth.*

—Bhagavad Gita

# Part II

# OM FACTOR RX:
## *7 Tools to Help in the Moment*

## Tool 1

# WHEN YOU FEEL OVERWHELMED

*"I need ten minutes . . . just ten minutes to myself."*

This plea to have just a few minutes for ourselves is heard across every continent, country, state, town, and home in this world. This statement, however, has one unique quality to it: You rarely hear it uttered by men. Even very successful men will say, "I am really busy or I don't have time," but you will rarely hear "I just need some time for *myself*" from a man.

Most women are taught directly, or have the underlying message conveyed to us, that our purpose on this earth is to be a good daughter and sister, and to then go on to be a good spouse and mother. We are taught to be the glue that holds the family together and to create a happy home. In previous generations parents rarely encouraged their daughters to follow their dreams to become whatever they chose to be.

Now, if they choose to be a housewife, CEO of a company, or an astronaut, it is perfectly acceptable, and they will be just as good if not better than their male counterparts. But still, the message is ***not*** to be one or the other. If you choose to work outside of the home you are still expected to be a good spouse and mother. Women do not get the hall pass that says, "But she is tired from working all day and therefore does not have to do the laundry, put dinner on the table, and make sure the children's backpacks are packed for the next day." It is expected that you will simply do it all.

Let's think about what happens with expectations. When we expect something from someone or something is expected from us, it puts stress or pressure on the other person or ourselves. These are the *external* demands placed by people who are outside of our physical body or demands we place on people outside of ourselves. If that is the case, then why is it that we as women feel the effects *internally*, within ourselves? I mean, that's not the way it's supposed to work, right? Unfortunately, *that is exactly how it works.*

***When you expect something from someone or something is expected from you, it actually produces a toxic response within your physical and emotional body.***

When you expect something from someone or something is expected from you, it actually produces a toxic response within your physical and emotional body. This goes for both women and men. Expectations are not gender based. However, interestingly, the *response* to placing them on someone or allowing them to be placed on you is very different in women when compared to men. In this situation where stress arises, we observe men and women handling the stress differently.

## What Is Stress?

Stress is a word that is used to describe experiences that are perceived to be challenging emotionally and physiologically. There is "good stress" and "bad stress." The good stress describes experiences that are for a finite and limited period of time and produce a sense of exhilaration and a feeling of accomplishment. "Bad stress," or when we say we are "stressed out or overwhelmed," refers to times when a sense of control of the situation is lacking, and stress is prolonged or recurrent. This becomes emotionally draining, physically exhausting, and ultimately dangerous.

"Women's reactions to stress are rooted in their body chemistry. Men have higher androgen levels, while women have higher estrogen levels, says Paul J. Rosch, MD, FACP, president of the American Institute of Stress (AIS). "Their brains are also wired differently," says Dr. Rosch, who is also a clinical professor of medicine and psychiatry at New York Medical College and honorary vice president of the International Stress Management Association. "Women tend to react to stress differently from men. They don't respond with the fight or flight response—they're more apt to negotiate."

Oddly, if women are more apt to negotiate, then why should there be prolonged stress manifested in our bodies and minds? Why isn't this good stress? Negotiation implies a win-win or "give-and-take" intention that is set at the onset so that both parties leave feeling whole and complete. That is negotiation in theory and perhaps it is negotiation in practice for some.

However, I believe that with a lot of women, negotiation means to "give in" and not "give," and certainly not to "take." There is not that equitable, harmonious exchange. Because we are taught to create harmony in our surroundings, we interpret that to mean that we must give up our desires and happiness in order to make others happy. This interpretation is detrimental and must change if we are to truly have harmony and peace within ourselves.

Let's look at these four words a little more closely: "give in" and "give up." The word "give" by itself has such a positive ring, meaning, and feeling associated with it. Your get a warm, fuzzy feeling in your heart. Your mind senses that you are doing something good, and we are all taught that giving is one of the best things you can do as a human being. You have a positive physical and mental response.

The moment you put the words "in" and "up" after "give," the meaning completely changes—and so does the physical manifestation. Your head drops down chin to chest, your shoulders cave in, and your mind feels like you have truly lost something. Well, you

***I believe that with a lot of women, negotiation means to "give in" and not "give," and certainly not to "take." There is not that equitable, harmonious exchange. Because we are taught to create harmony in our surroundings, we interpret that to mean that we must give up our desires and happiness in order to make others happy.***

have. You have not only lost that particular thing you wanted, but there is a real physical manifestation of this stressful feeling within your body and it affects all of your systems.

Then, we as women do something that truly boggles the mind. As if digesting that feeling once was not good enough, we replay the event over and over again, turning that one occurrence into many incidents, and the downward spiral begins. We go to the doctor with unexplainable symptoms; we receive a battery of tests, and unless there is a concrete diagnosis we hear this familiar refrain: "It's probably just stress." Sometimes, we even say this to ourselves to rationalize not going to see the doctor to follow up on our distressful symptoms.

Stress is really not something one should ignore. It truly affects every system in your body and no body part is spared. I feel compelled to talk about this here because as women we tend to ignore or minimize symptoms because we quite frankly "just don't have time to fit it in."

To really understand how bad this is, take a few minutes and peruse the following list of eleven major effects of stress on our bodies and nervous system. There are many more, but this list will give you a very clear idea as to the pervasiveness and global impact that stress has on us. See how many of these feelings and ailments you are currently experiencing or have experienced.

Unfortunately, most of you will be nodding your head in recognition as you go down this list. Those who don't can flip through the rest of the book and enjoy the wonderful poetry and continue their clearly evolved and well-established practice of meditation!

## Eleven Ways Stress Affects Your Body and Mind

### 1. Weight Gain

When we feel stressed out, a lot of us develop cravings for salty, fatty, and sugary foods to help us feel better. That is why they are called comfort foods. It's great to feel better, and there are studies that show that eating these comfort foods make a temporary difference. However, the word "temporary" is key. The more you feel stressed, the more you will eat, and then the effect no longer becomes temporary. The shocking thing is that even with a healthy diet you can gain weight—especially in your midsection. The release of cortisol, which is a big stress hormone, appears to boost abdominal fat. Cortisol and Insulin also appear to be the cause of stress-related food cravings. The problem is that it is not just confined to our belly's getting bigger. Abdominal fat really increases the risk of diabetes and heart problems.

### 2. Broken Heart

I mean this literally. Acute stress immediately causes an increase in your heart rate, and your heart muscle contracts more strongly. Your blood vessels begin to dilate and the amount of blood pumped to your heart and the larger muscles increases. This can cause inflammation in the coronary arteries and result in a heart attack with repeated episodes of stress. There is also a strong role that stress can play in hypertension or high blood pressure as your heart beats faster and your blood vessels narrow.

According to a July 2012 study conducted by Dr. Michelle Albert, a professor in cardiovascular medicine at Brigham and Women's Hospital, stressful jobs increased the risk of heart attack in women by an astonishing 70 percent. She and her colleagues analyzed data from over 22,000 women over the span of ten years. The data was derived from asking women questions about their sense of control they felt at work and job strain. Although many of us cannot leave our current jobs for our dream jobs due to our circumstances, we can absolutely control the way we feel about our lives and find happiness in any situation. Once this organ stops working, the game is over.

### 3. Reproductive Function Problems

Stress is known to affect hormone levels. As a result, a woman under high stress may find that she has less frequent or even missed periods. Periods can also become more painful. Symptoms of PMS and menopause have been reported to worsen with stress. Hormonal imbalances caused by stress may make the symptoms of endometriosis and fibroid tumors worse.

Furthermore, stress can also affect fertility. According to some sources, the chemical changes that stress induces in the body can affect the maturation and release of the egg. It can also cause spasms in the fallopian tubes and uterus, affecting implantation. This actually applies to both men and women as stress in men can affect sperm count and motility. Then, infertility itself causes more stress. The stress of desperately wanting a child and not being able to have one, the efforts to determine the root of the problem of not being able to conceive, and the painful and emotionally draining treatments are only a few of the results of hormonal imbalance. Truly, stress begets stress.

### 4. Digestive System Problems

Stress-related symptoms may also include constipation, diarrhea, heartburn, bloating, and stomach cramps. Tension can also cause other gastrointestinal disorders such as irritable bowel syndrome, which is very strongly related to emotional stress. This is a condition when the large intestine gets very irritated, and instead of the smooth wave-like contractions that it normally has, it has spastic contractions. The abdomen becomes bloated and the person experiences bouts of alternating constipation and diarrhea.

### 5. Rashes

Believe it or not, your skin can tell you a lot about your stress level. Stress can cause breakouts of itchy rashes with raised spots or hives on the face, stomach, arms, and back. Experts say that stress releases histamine, which causes the itchy bumps.

### 6. Headaches

Tension headaches are the most common form of headache and women are twice as likely as men to get them. Usually this kind of headache is caused by tense muscles in the scalp and neck, and you feel the pain around the forehead or back of the head and neck. These can really interrupt your day, whether the pain is debilitating or not. Sometimes the headaches don't start until long after the stressful event or interaction has ended. Many studies show that emotional stress is also a possible trigger for more severe migraine headaches even though the headache may show up after the acute stress has subsided.

### 7. Trouble Falling Asleep and Staying Asleep

People often hear the word insomnia and think it means that you have to be unable to sleep the entire night to have it. That is not the case. If you have trouble falling asleep or staying asleep, it's a form of insomnia. We have all been there. We turn off the light looking forward to a few hours of deeply needed shut-eye and . . . nothing. But our brains are in overdrive thinking about that project we need to complete, bills we need to pay, the person we need to talk with, and a million other things. This is unfortunately very common. Studies show that 70 percent of adults with chronic stress have trouble sleeping. This also creates a vicious cycle. You are stressed because you can't sleep, and then the next day you are stressed because you didn't get sleep the night before. As a result, you are again sleepy and exhausted the following day.

### 8. Trouble Concentrating

Stress can make it really hard to focus and be effective in your daily life. Handling all of your responsibilities becomes very overwhelming, and you are a lot less successful at completing that "to-do" list. It can also cause confusion when you can't make seemingly easy and routine decisions, such as what to make for dinner or which outfit to wear to work the next day.

### 9. Forgetting Things

How many times have you lost your keys or left your cell phone somewhere? How many times have you missed a meeting or forgotten to pick up something you had been reminded to do only a few hours before? Countless times in most cases. Many studies have connected long-term exposure to stress to the shrinking of the hippocampus, that is the brain's memory center. The good news: research also shows that once the stress level comes back to normal, the size of the memory center also follows suit. But who wants to shrink ANY part of their brain, even if it's for a little while?

### 10. Weakening of the Immune System

Do you get sick often? If so, you may want to really rethink all that worrying you are doing. Your immune system gets a huge knockout punch when stress attacks it. There was a study conducted at the Medical Research Council's Cold Unit in England led by researcher Sheldon Cohen. Researchers injected a cold virus in to 394 volunteers, and those who reported that they didn't have much stress in their lives had such strong immune systems that they were half as likely to get sick as the other volunteers who reported that they had very high stress levels. People that have chronic stress have low white blood cell counts due to the shrinking of their thymus gland, which is responsible for making those cells. This then makes them more susceptible to infection. Also, once you get a cold, stress can really impair your body's ability to fight off the infection.

**11. Jaw Pain and Cavities**

Who would have thought that cavities were related to stress? I was always told that it was because I ate too much candy. But since the stress from your day doesn't magically disappear at night, women tend to unknowingly grind their teeth a lot at night. This actually erodes their teeth, making them very susceptible to cavities. In really severe cases doing this often can leave you with teeth that are worn down to nubs, and in most cases it causes jaw pain and headaches. A night guard from a dentist can help this, but why not just resolve the stress—or better yet, as we'll learn how in the tools described in the chapters ahead, reduce the incidents of feeling stressed and hopefully eventually eliminate them.

While all these symptoms are stress related, nothing said here is meant to replace seeing or getting the advice of your physician. On the contrary, if you are experiencing any of these symptoms, take them seriously and follow up with your doctor.

Picture a beautiful clear vase filled with refreshingly cool water. Add to this water one drop of blue food coloring. One drop tints the water only very lightly. As you add more drops, the water gets darker and darker and eventually it is almost opaque. The reason that one drop only tints it lightly is because the majority of the water is clear. It is only when an abundance of color is added that a real difference is seen. It's the same thing with our bodies. A minimal amount of stress will not have the consequences that a great amount of stress does. With constant and consistent stress, you won't even recognize the woman in the mirror anymore. You will be left to ask, if you have not already, the timeless question: "What happened to me and how did I get here?"

## Rx to Heal Feelings of Being Overwhelmed

Women's lives are one big balancing act. Imagine walking on a tightrope, carrying enough items that you need four arms, but you only have two. Not only must you not drop anything, but you must look graceful as you do this.

Meditation practiced preventatively each day, and the use of mantras or affirmations during acute situations, gives you those two extra arms. These enable you to access the creativity space within your soul to be able to organize your time and relationships so that all the items fit nicely. The act of repeating the mantra or affirmation stops the bleeding until you can truly heal the wound by practicing meditation either in the morning before your day officially starts or in the evening before you retire, or both.

When feeling overwhelmed, repeat the following affirmation quietly or silently:

*This too shall pass*

OR

*Om Shanti Shanti Shanti*

*(Om Peace, Peace, Peace)*

Whether you are feeling overwhelmed from the various deadlines/deliverables and endless meetings at work, or from shuttling the kids back and forth to activities while having to manage all the household demands, or from dealing with challenging relationships in your home or work environments, these affirmations and mantras will certainly help you when you are feeling that sense of pressure.

***Women's lives are one big balancing act. Imagine walking on a tightrope, carrying enough items that you need four arms, but you only have two. Not only must you not drop anything, but you must look graceful as you do this.***

Then, when you awaken every morning, try sitting in silence to not only set the tone and intention of the day, but to also repair any damage that has been done from negative thoughts, the environment, or the stresses and pressures of your daily life. Remember, it does not matter how long you sit. Ideally, if you can build up to twenty minutes or longer, this is great. If not, even two minutes makes a profound difference. What matters is consistency. If you are able, try to also sit in silence in the evening or just before you retire if time does not permit this earlier in the day. During this time you also may choose to recite a mantra, affirmation, or simply observe the breath. This is a personal choice.

### *Healing Gemstone: Angelite*

Angelite is a stone that can bring serenity, inner peace, and a sense of calm. Angelite is great to use when you need to calm down from feelings of stress and being overwhelmed. You may put this stone in your purse or pocket and also have it on your desk in front of you to draw on its powerful properties.

*Immediate Steps to Take When Feeling Overwhelmed*

- Take clear mental and physical notes of the seemingly unimportant coincidences that unfold in your life.
- Take a deep breath.
- Quietly or silently begin repeating the mantra or affirmation.
- Observe the change in yourself and the situation.

## 7 Daily Steps to Healing the Wound and Getting Your Two Extra Arms

1. Find a quiet place.
2. Close your eyes.
3. *Observe* your breath.
4. *Do not judge your thoughts if you have them. Let them come and go.*
5. Repeat your mantra or affirmation if you wish, as if you are listening to it.
6. Picture what you are trying to manifest.
7. Let it go and continue steps 3-5 for whatever time you are able to sit.

# THE GUEST HOUSE

*This being human is a guest house.*
*Every morning a new arrival.*

*A joy, a depression, a meanness,*
*some momentary awareness comes*
*as an unexpected visitor.*

*Welcome and entertain them all!*
*Even if they're a crowd of sorrows,*
*who violently sweep your house*
*empty of its furniture,*
*still, treat each guest honorably.*
*He may be clearing you out*
*for some new delight.*

*The dark thought, the shame, the malice,*
*meet them at the door laughing,*
*and invite them in.*

*Be grateful for whoever comes,*
*because each has been sent*
*as a guide from beyond.*

—RUMI,
*Translation by Coleman Barks*

Tool 2

# WHEN YOU FEEL INADEQUATE

Here is the dirty little secret that women don't talk about. We have all either experienced this or heard it from another: the sense that we are not worthy, we are imposters, and we will be found out. We feel that we are frauds. The reason this is not talked about is that when you are promoted to a leadership role, or find yourself in such a role by default, you are expected to know what to do and do it gracefully. Showing any type of hesitation is perceived as a sign of weakness. We feel that if we show any type of indecisiveness, vacillation, or doubt our employees, children, or anyone that we are leading will not respect us and mutiny will set in. That is a very doomsday-like and dramatic assumption, and one that is probably untrue.

***The key to successful leadership is to inspire others by tuning into their individual vibration and aligning it with that of the goal. This means leadership has nothing, absolutely nothing, to do with the type of person you are or your strengths or shortcomings. That perception is completely ego based.***

But the key to successful leadership is to inspire others by tuning into their individual vibration and aligning it with that of the goal. This means leadership has nothing, absolutely nothing, to do with the type of person you are or your strengths or shortcomings. That perception is completely ego based.

According to Webster's Dictionary the ego is "The "I" or self of any person; a person as thinking, feeling, and willing and distinguishing itself from the selves of others." Everything that ego-based persons think about their identity come from things that are outside of themselves, such as physical appearance, possessions, social stature, failures, successes, what they do for a living, and political affiliation, etc. These are a way to answer the question "Who am I?" without having to open yourself to the person asking about you, or, even more importantly, really knowing who you truly are—your essence.

It is an easy way to hide by simply saying, "I am a Project Manager at a Big 4 Consulting firm," or "I am a mother" or "I am the CEO of a Fortune 100 company." The ego-based mind feels comfortable in this space—the space of a self-painted reality onto the canvas of perceived existence. The ego-mind uses whichever colors, textures, or shapes it fancies that enable it to feel in control and safe.

If you are surrounded by a group of mothers you may choose to say, "I am a mother to three beautiful children and a member of Junior League." If you are at a networking event you may choose to say, "I am the CFO of a large pharmaceutical firm, live in McLean, Virginia, and I am very involved in these particular charities." Both of those descriptions look beautiful on the canvas that you painted, and both are very different. Both also describe you in a light that appears to be flattering. You feel a self-created sense of acceptance, and if you are lucky, even that you are liked.

***The ego-mind is fueled and sustained by fear, insecurity, and the desire to be accepted. As long as these things exist, the ego-mind will continue to thrive.***

It is extremely important for the ego-mind to be liked and respected. The fact that all of these sensations and feelings are an illusion and what is transient does not matter to the ego-mind. The ego-mind is fueled and sustained by fear, insecurity, and the desire to be accepted. As long as these things exist, the ego-mind will continue to thrive.

## True Leadership

When we live at the level and vibration of the ego-mind we cannot possibly be connected to God. We cannot even be in the presence of God. Spirit, or the soul, or divine consciousness cannot survive at this level or vibration. Being connected to God at the spiritual level of our higher selves allows us to detach from our ego-based self so that we can lead more effectively. The most effective leaders are fully aware that it is not about them; it is about inspiring others to be their best selves.

So, in effect, true leadership is not the act of leading, but is rather cultivating the fertile ground within others. Both the noise of self-doubt, insecurity, and fear, and the silence of the absence of love and light, are deafening. This literally, as thought leaders have said, "*Edges God Out.*" In other words, you will never get the true answer to "Who am I?" or be able to answer "Who are you?" until you live at the level of spirit.

***True leadership is not the act of leading, but is rather cultivating the fertile ground within others.***

Many people, because of their social and religious conditioning, believe that their connection to God is external. For them God is creativity. God is love. God is compassion. God is the universe and everything we perceive. But do all these things not come from within you, from your highest self? Have you ever felt like you were completely on top of your game or that you were making a difference in the world at large or in your world? Have you found yourself feeling like everything is happening effortlessly and harmoniously and that you just flow?

These feelings or sensations are felt by those who are in the presence of Grace or God. At this time they are experiencing the OM Factor. They understand that in order to manifest that which they desire they must connect with their highest selves, and the answers are always within and come from having that dialogue which takes place by going into silence. It's that gap between thought A and thought B. They are connected with the vibration that creates the universe. They are enveloped in that vibration, and they radiate that vibration to everyone that comes into contact with them.

People are magnetically drawn to them and they are immensely attractive. They rarely need to think about what to do next. It just comes to them. Love just exudes from them without discretion—to every sentient being. We all know people like these. Are you one of them? If you are not, do you want to be? It is as simple as turning the lights on in a dark room. You must make a conscious choice to navigate through unchartered waters and embrace uncertainty. This is the only real way of reaching enlightenment or manifesting your deepest intentions.

Successful leadership has *everything* to do with the individual that is right in front of you. This is the most important person at that moment. I believe that having one style of leadership is not effective and is potentially counter-productive. Having just one style will be effective for leading those who resonate with that vibration, but not for leadership of the entire group and certainly not for every individual.

We are used to hearing, "She's a tough cookie; don't get on her bad side." Or, "Oh, he's a really nice guy; just make sure you do what he says." Those are stereotypical perceptions that become the trademarks of leaders when masses of people believe them to be true. They are so powerful that the leader herself or himself begins to believe this to be their style, and it becomes a self-fulfilling prophecy. That does not benefit anyone. Leadership is showing others the art of the possible. It's inspiring others to dream without boundaries and to instill confidence to believe that those dreams can actually be manifested.

## Lessons from a Horse

I learned something quite interesting while a on a retreat to Miraval Resort & Spa in Tucson, Arizona. They have a signature experience called the Equine Experience. This was fascinating to me. We learned many things about grooming a horse, ranging from cleaning their hoofs to brushing their mane. We learned how to approach a horse: never right in front of its face, but rather to the side of it. However, when all was said and done we really learned a lot about ourselves as well as about life. There were two things that stood out to me while participating in this enlightening experience.

First was the *seemingly* simple task of picking out or cleaning a horse's hoof. There is a special place three quarters of the way down the horse's leg that you must grip pretty firmly in order for the horse to lift its leg, giving you access to pick out the dirt and debris from its hoof. I had never been around a horse in my life, but was very open to the experience. Or, so I thought.

I walked up to the horse and started talking to him and told him that I would really appreciate it if he could lift up his leg so I could clean his hoof. I then cupped my hand around his ankle and squeezed to give the cue for him to lift his leg. Nothing happened. His knees were totally locked, and there wasn't even a slight gesture of lifting the leg. I was stunned. I was being friendly and charming, I thought. I informed him of what was about to happen so that he could be prepared, and then I executed it. I did another few iterations of this and each time tried to make a slight adjustment.

The horse instructor, or whisperer in my opinion, was watching me from afar and came over and asked me how I get people to do what I need them to in my daily life? I told her that I try to establish a connection and then when I feel that they are on board we execute the plan or tasks we have put in place. I also told her when that didn't work, I would take a step back and reassess and approach it a different way—all of which I did the multiple times I tried approaching my horse.

She told me that horses can sense many things and that telling a horse that it is beautiful and asking it to do something is not the way a horse responds. The horse responds when you walk up with a sense of purpose, grab the ankle purposefully and go about your business of cleaning. She walked up and did it in the first go. I was astonished. Could the horse sense any insincerity or anxiety in my presence or even in my space when I walked up to him?

I needed to understand that the horse communicated and learned by feeling that I was clear in my objective and that I could just execute it. No hesitations, even subtle ones, would work here. I then approached the horse as if I had already cleaned his hoof dozens of times, and it worked! I learned what he needed, walked up with commitment and purpose, and we both achieved our goals. This was eye-opening, and my horse provided a mirror to my style of leadership and how I dealt with people in my daily life.

I immediately wanted to rush back to the office and apply what I had learned with my staff and see if it still would have the same outcome. So, during our weekly and sometimes daily "state of the union" meetings at Technalink, and during our annual reviews, I decided to focus more on the things that my employees could improve on and less on making sure that I had enough positive reinforcement in there to "buffer" the constructive criticism.

I always thought that when you are delivering news that may be bitter tasting at first, you should perhaps coat it with some honey so that it goes down smoother and the experience is more palatable. That is really not the case. People respond to mutual respect more than they do to sugar coating. They want to know that they are respected and valued and hear where they can improve constructively along with some kudos. The kudos does not need to come first. Just be a straight-shooter.

The second task that stood out had an even more profound effect on me. When training a horse with a longing whip you are supposed to stand *behind* the horse in order to lead it. This actually worked. The horse knew exactly where the leader wanted it to go, but still had the freedom to move and execute this in its own manner. The leader speeds up her pace, and the horse speeds up; the leader slows down and so does the horse.

However, the leader never maintains a position of being directly in front of the horse with the horse physically following her. You need to not only stand behind the horse, but also turn your feet to a forty-five-degree angle in order to line up your abdomen (power center) with that of the horse's rear, which is where its power center is.

This is counterintuitive in the workplace, or in life for that matter. Captains stand at the helm of a ship, a parent is called "the head" of the family, the king and queen stand upon their balcony with their subjects below and before them, and CEOs and Managers are all at the head of the boardroom table. All these people are leaders and all of them are physically positioned and also semantically referred to as "the head" or "chief" or "leader."

***When leading, give people room to move and be and have their own journey while showing them where you want to go. You do not have to be in someone's face to lead them.***

When leading, give people room to move and be and have their own journey while showing them where you want to go. You do not have to be in someone's face to lead them. *Align your energy with theirs and it all flows.*

Take the time to sit down and find out what their personal desires are and what their ideas are on how to accomplish something. Really listen, and with an open mind you might realize and be surprised that there may be a better way to achieve the goal, and it might even change the entire landscape of what was originally thought. Those people that you are leading then become fully invested in achieving your vision, and they also feel a true part of the whole, rather than just feeling like it's a job where they show up to punch in and punch out while their minds, thoughts, feelings, and intentions are elsewhere.

When we are in harmony with each other, that is when results are achieved. We do not all have to play the same instrument or the same beat, but we all do have to be in harmony. When we do that, the universe aligns itself to manifest our desired outcome.

> "Everything is energy and that is all there is to it. Match the frequency of the reality you want and you cannot help but get that reality. It can be no other way. This is not philosophy. This is physics."
>
> —quotation widely attributed to Albert Einstein

Because women are a nurturing species, listening to and aligning with others comes easily to them. Women are collaborative and also communicative by nature, so these conversations come naturally and are often very productive. Women need to remember that by going with the flow of their nature of being good listeners, nurturing, and encouraging, does not make them weak or less than anyone or anything. This is a true strength and one that should be used to its fullest in a leadership position. The sun can give nourishment and strength and warmth without ever depleting itself. It still remains the single most powerful source of life and energy in the universe. While providing so much to all sentient beings, it self-renews and self-sustains.

## Rx to Heal Feelings of Inadequacy

When feeling inadequate or challenged say the following affirmation quietly or silently:

*I am being divinely guided.*

OR

*Om Namah Shivaya*

The affirmation, "I am being divinely guided" is very powerful. When you repeat this affirmation, your subtle body and soul recalibrate immediately as the words "I am" and "divinely" inject God into the equation. Your highest self-God is guiding you through this journey through life. Regardless of whatever your personal definition of God is, where God exists there is never any inadequacy or deficiency. There is only abundance and prosperity.

When you feel the vibration of your highest self through the sounds of repeating this affirmation you will soon notice that your feelings of being unsure or inadequate will start to wane, and you will feel a sense of confidence and strength come over you. It's as if you have the map to the Holy Grail in your hand, and the road ahead is open and inviting. Anyone that you are leading will recalibrate with you when you do this.

The mantra "Om Namah Shivaya," pronounced (Aum Num-ha Shi-Va-Ya), is a very powerful mantra. This vibration and the sounds of this mantra relate directly to the principles that govern each of the first six chakras on the spine: earth, water, fire, air, and ether. The six syllables of the chant represent the first six chakras that run from the root of the spine (muladhara chakra) to the third eye (ajna chakra).

This mantra's vibrations cleanse all five elements that are present in the body. It also cleanses the environment that surrounds you. The phrasing and the energy of the sounds are designed to create a shift in your consciousness and enables you to attain a higher state of awareness.

Shiva is the bestower of inner strength, fearlessness, consciousness, and detachment. Shiva is the supreme reality, the inner self. The literal translation is, "I bow to Shiva, who is the higher self within all of us, who is pure unconditional love and pure bliss." One meaning of the translation of this mantra is "I honor my inner divine self." You may do this mantra with the mala (108 beads) when you do your meditation, or you can also use it when you are in an acute situation where you feel inadequate, have self-depreciating thoughts, or feel challenged.

When you repeat this mantra a re-circuiting of the brain happens and you will feel your energy level shift, leaving you feeling empowered and knowing that the divine within you is present and all is well. I repeat this mantra every day, as it is very powerful and cleansing and restorative at the same time.

### *Healing Gemstone: Carnelian*

Carnelian is a self-esteem crystal that can be used to help eliminate feelings of inadequacy and low self-esteem. The deep orange colors of carnelian blend the 1st, 2nd and 3rd chakras very nicely to promote and encourage self-love and self-security. This is great for recovery after rejection. You may put this stone in your pocket or your purse and/or on your desk.

### *Immediate Steps to Take When Feeling Inadequate in a Leadership Role*

- Take a deep breath.
- Quietly or silently begin repeating the mantra or affirmation.
- Observe the change in yourself and the situation.

## 7 Daily Steps to Healing the Wound

1. Find a quiet place.
2. Close your eyes.
3. *Observe* your breath.
4. *Do not be judgmental if you have thoughts. Let them come and go.*
5. Repeat your mantra or affirmation if you wish, as if you are listening to it.
6. Picture what you are trying to manifest.
7. Let it go and continue steps 3-5 for whatever time you are able to sit.

# THE YOGA OF WORKS

*Every selfless act, Arjuna,*
*is born from Brahman,*
*the eternal, infinite Godhead.*
*He is present in every act of service.*
*All life turns on this law, O Arjuna.*
*Whoever violates it,*
*indulging his senses for his own pleasure*
*and ignoring the needs of others,*
*has wasted his life.*

*But those who realize the Self*
*are always satisfied.*
*Having found the source of*
*joy and fulfillment,*
*they no longer seek happiness*
*from the external world.*
*They have nothing to gain*
*or lose by any action;*
*neither people nor things*
*can affect their security.*

*Strive constantly to serve*
*the welfare of the world;*
*by devotion to selfless work one*
*attains the supreme goal of life.*
*Do your work with the*
*welfare of others always in mind*

—Bhagavad Gita

## Tool 3

# WHEN YOU FEEL ANXIOUS

### Where Your Mind Goes, Energy Flows

HOW MANY TIMES HAVE YOU THOUGHT *I hope that person doesn't call, I hope that person doesn't call, I hope that person doesn't* . . . And THEY CALL. You actually kept repeating it. You manifested that. You put your energy/focus on that and it happened. When you focus on the negative aspects of something they also are manifested, although that it is not what you wanted to happen.

Your thoughts are energy. When that energy comes from a positive place and one of love, compassion, and abundance the outcome you desire is manifested. When the energy comes from a place of anxiety or worry the opposite happens. If you ever doubted the strength of a mantra, this should resonate with you and render you a believer.

Now, imagine if we didn't "worry" about what was going to happen, but rather enjoyed what was happening and were totally present. Then it's like fireworks on the fourth of July! Everything becomes awe inspiring. Everything looks amazing and beautiful. You are almost waiting with bated breath for the next set of fireworks to appear. Will they be red, green, or blue? Will there be shapes of smiley faces? I wonder what they will decide to do next? What will we see? That is the type of wonder that we need to move throughout our lives with.

Children have this sense of wonder. Everything is a masterpiece to them, and they flow through their activities and just enjoy life and take it all in like they are soaking up the sun on a beautiful day. This sense of wonder is what makes our deepest desires and intentions manifest. If you perceived everything as fireworks imagine what your world would look and feel like? Imagine what our collective world would look and feel like and then further imagine what our universe would look like. A Utopia could emerge.

Children do have that sense of wonder, don't they? They are pretty oblivious to anxiety as far as an objective observer can perceive, and they basically are simply enjoying being. There is no sign of anxiety hovering over waiting to pounce on its prey. However, at some point anxiety thrusts its sharp talons into their bodies piercing their souls. When does it change? When do we go from being carefree to feeling plagued with, at times, debilitating anxiety? Is it when you are age five, ten, thirteen, or twenty? Is it different for boys versus girls?

## How Our Perception of Past Events Affects Future Anxiety

Two fascinating studies were conducted in 2007 by the Society for Research in Child Development* demonstrating the **belief** that both a certain and **potential** reoccurrence of a negative event from the past can cause anxiety and preventative behaviors. The results of this research contributed to our understanding about why females engage in more worrying about events, have less tolerance for uncertainty, perceive more risk in situations, and therefore experience anxiety at a higher rate than males.

Both studies involved one hundred twenty-eight people: three- to six-year-olds as well as adults. The first study had the participants listen to several stories where the characters in the story had

* Source: http://www.science20.com: "Anxiety in Females: How Perception of the Past Impacts the Present. Based on studies Society for Research in Child Development, October 2, 2007.

experienced negative events with people or animals. In the several days following the negative events, the characters were experiencing real anxiety and modified their behavior when they came into contact with the people/animals that caused them pain. This seems like a very natural and logical feeling that would come over most people when they come face to face with someone that causes them pain. In fact, this is not surprising at all.

After hearing the stories, the children and adults in the study were then asked to explain why the characters acted worried or changed their behavior and then predict how a character that had not experienced the prior negative event would react in a similar situation. The second study was identical to the first except that the perpetrator in the final scene only *appeared similar* to the one that had actually hurt them in the past.

In both studies, the female adults and children explained the characters reactions to be caused by the *potential* harm or the *possibility* of harm rather than the certainty of harm being eminent. The female adults and children also predicted that even when the perpetrator was *similar* to and not the same person that caused the characters harm, they would still feel incredible anxiety. They felt that the mere resemblance would trigger the fear of the same thing happening to them that happened in the past.

"Both studies clearly found that children and adults both believe that negative past events forecast negative future events, even when the perpetrator only *resembles* the past person that harmed them." It was also observed that children somewhere between three and six years old can begin to understand that feelings of anxiety and fear can be directly caused by the thought of a negative event from the past *potentially* reoccurring. They are also aware that those who didn't experience or weren't aware of the negative past would probably feel and act very differently. So, there we have it: from three to six years of age is when we become cognizant of anxiety and its effect.

It should be noted that boys and men in these studies also provided explanations about the relationship of their past experiences to their anticipation of future events. They, however, did not believe that negative past events predicted future events as frequently as the girls and women did.

Could this study perhaps help to explain why we typecast certain people we encounter for the first time in business meetings/negotiations or in the workplace as "challenging," "self-centered," "demanding," or "overbearing"? We make these determinations sometimes based on a thirty-second encounter or sometimes even just by looking at them. We may get all geared-up inside to deal with these individuals based on our past encounters with *similarly appearing* people.

Perhaps we had dealt with an overbearing co-worker, demanding client, or self-centered boss and have efficiently typecast our newest victim of our protective branding without skipping a beat. We have all felt the anxiety of meeting people for the first time with our preconceived notions of what we think they will be like or, even worse, meeting with individuals whom we have known for years and have type-casted them based on our uncomfortable interactions with them. This last statement raises a question. Were these individuals whom we have known for years causing our internal anxiety truly "overbearing" or "demanding," or did our initial opinion of them just stick and we didn't give them a fighting chance to be something other than what we were afraid they were based on someone that they reminded us of?

***When the same issues seem to arise, realize there is a lesson you must learn to break the cycle. The universe mirrors it back until you get it.***

When the same issues seem to arise, realize there is a lesson you must learn to break the cycle. The universe mirrors it back until you get it. This is very prevalent in our emotional relationships. We often feel that the man or woman who reached inside and ripped our hearts out, only leaving scraps of plasma as a souvenir, will manifest themselves in every other man or woman that we meet.

Here our anxiety of the past is sabotaging our future. You know this when you wonder why you keep meeting the same type of woman or man over and over and over again. That's exactly why. You and your anxiety are manifesting these persons and they will show up again and again until you learn the lesson.

Anxiety puts up a barrier to achieving your goals and is self-defeating. When we find ourselves bemoaning all the awful things that *could* happen if we don't satisfy that client, if we don't get the project done on time, or if we aren't a "good enough" mother, we then create the very reality we fear. By creating a future reality that has not happened you are creating a present that is unbearable to live in. But when we live fully in the present with the knowledge that we are supported by the universe, anxiety ceases to exist.

***By creating a future reality that has not happened you are creating a present that is unbearable to live in. But when we live fully in the present with the knowledge that we are supported by the universe, anxiety ceases to exist.***

## Rx to Heal Feelings of Anxiety

When feeling anxiety say the following affirmation quietly or silently:

*I am supported.*

OR

*Om Gam Ganpathaye Namaha*

The affirmation "I am supported" is so powerful. This affirmation immediately brings a sense of strength and confidence to your being when recited. Just as the trunk of the tree is supporting its branches, you are supported. This affirmation is invoking the support of the universal energy to corral around you and bring an immediate sense of calm and strength. When we feel support as human beings we are less anxious or fearful of any obstacles that may appear in front of us. We feel that we can overcome anything and things are really not so bad.

You may have felt this sense of confidence when you thought that a coworker backed your ideas in a meeting, or if you had some additional expenses come up in life or in business and you had an adequate line of credit to deal with them. This feeling of support changes the entire outcome of the situation by changing the way that we perceive it. We as human beings thirst for the feeling of being supported, as it fortifies our spirit and enables us to feel as though we can conquer the world.

One of the biggest complaints of women in the workplace or in life in general is that they do not feel supported in one or both places. Whether caused by a situation of competition, jealousy, or the feeling of not being heard or taken seriously, this causes anxiety as we feel that the very foundation that we exist on is not secure or solid. This feeling of having support is not something that comes with your annual raise at work. It is a feeling that is cultivated by inner strength as well as healthy, nurturing relationships both at home and in the workplace.

True collaboration can bring about a strong sense of being supported. When we collaborate everyone is vested. Everyone is working towards the same goal. Everyone feels heard and taken seriously. Jealousy and competitiveness wither away as everyone is working towards the same goal and have a common thread bonding them together. In a most collaborations, there is a leader that emerges somewhat organically, and sometimes that can feel threatening as one may perceive there to be an agenda of some sort.

However, when we realize that the leader is merely another part of the whole and plays a certain role that is not superior to any other role, this feeling will subside. Everyone plays a role in all collaborations and relationships. Everyone's role is equally important in order to achieve the collective goal and also a sense of balance and harmony. No one is inferior or superior to anyone else in this world. This is a universal truth that is often ignored and misunderstood because of ego.

***We as human beings thirst for the feeling of being supported, as it fortifies our spirit and enables us to feel as though we can conquer the world. One of the biggest complaints of women in the workplace or in life in general is that they do not feel supported in one or both places.***

Even if you were not blessed with a strong family unit, supportive parents, or currently in an emotionally supportive situation, everyone can access universal support at any time. That support is omnipresent and infinite. Invoking this support through this affirmation is not something that has to be done during meditation. It can be accessed at any time. Invoke universal support with this affirmation and marvel at the outcome.

The Hindu God Ganesh is the remover of all obstacles. His association with obstacles comes from the great strength of the elephant combined with the intelligence of the human being since Ganesh is half man and half elephant. We all know that hardships and difficulties are a part of life and will always arrive, but it is how we perceive and deal with them that matters. If there are no perceived obstacles, there is then nothing to feel anxious about. This mantra can help resolve many problems and anxieties. It works to bring about unity between our desire and the object of our desire.

Because of this it is also the mantra of success and prosperity. The mantra OM Gam Ganpathaye Namaha, (pronounced Aum-Gum-Gun-Patha-Yei-Na-Ma-Ha), can be used whenever you are feeling anxiety of any kind, including before starting any endeavor like a new job or new business career, or engaging in a new contract or deal in order to remove any obstacles in your path and arrive at the final destination of success.

The vibration of this mantra resonates mostly in the first or mooladhara chakra. It is from this chakra that all the other upper chakras are supported and guided. I recite this mantra 108 times every day in the morning as part of my daily meditation practice with a mala. It has significantly impacted my life in a very positive way, both in my outlook on life as well as finding life experiences that I enjoy.

I would like to point out at this time that when reciting the mantras in Sanskrit this is not chanting them to a particular deity, but rather chanting them to *invoke* the characteristics and the qualities that they embody. This will assuage those who feel *anxiety* because of conflicting beliefs or religions. Both the affirmation and the mantra have the same effect and can be used as you wish. Do what feels comfortable to you.

### *Healing Gemstone: Rose Quartz*

This is known as the love stone. Rose quartz helps to unblock anxiety and also helps with healing of private emotional issues. Rose quartz helps to calm people down, which reduces stress and anxiety. It eases guilt and balances emotions. Whenever you feel anxiety coming on, hold the rose quartz in your hand and hold it up to your heart center for a few minutes, and you will feel the anxiety slowly going away. As an added bonus this stone helps with relationship issues, attracting love and bringing love and openness to the situation. You can keep this in your purse or on your desk at work.

### *Healing Gemstone: Flourite*

Because anxiety is such a prevalent emotion that plagues many people I have decided to include a second stone as well that is incredibly effective at diffusing anxiety. This multi-colored stone is fondly referred to as the "worry stone." Holding and rubbing it's smooth surface in your hand when feeling anxiety come on is very calming as the stone is known to absorb and neutralize negative vibrations. There is usually an indentation for the thumb and it is thus held between the thumb and the index finger. It also increases concentration and is very helpful in decision making as well. The other thing that is great about this stone is that it helps to remove the emotional involvement from the situation so you can see things with more clarity.

### *Immediate Steps to Take When Feeling Anxious*

- Take a deep breath.
- Quietly or silently begin repeating the mantra or affirmation.
- Observe the change in yourself and the situation.

## Daily Steps to Healing the Wound

1. Find a quiet place.
2. Close your eyes.
3. *Observe* your breath.
4. *Do not be judgmental if you have thoughts. Let them come and go.*
5. Repeat your mantra or affirmation if you wish, as if you are listening to it.
6. Picture what you are trying to manifest.
7. Let it go and continue steps 3-5 for whatever time you are able to sit.

# WHERE THE MIND IS WITHOUT FEAR

*Where the mind is without fear and the head is held high*

*Where knowledge is free*

*Where the world has not been broken up into fragments*

*By narrow domestic walls*

*Where words come out from the depth of truth*

*Where tireless striving stretches its arms towards perfection*

*Where the clear stream of reason has not lost its way*

*Into the dreary desert sand of dead habit*

*Where the mind is led forward by thee*

*Into ever-widening thought and action*

*Into that heaven of freedom, my Father, let my country awake*

—Rabindranath Tagore

Tool 4

# WHEN YOU FEEL INDECISIVE

Women are champion second-guessers. For example, we decide to hire someone and then question whether we made the right choice. Was the other candidate stronger, would the other candidate be a better fit, did I interview enough people? It does not take a rocket scientist to know that none of those questions are productive, yet we constantly ask them in our thought clouds, and they circle around like a tornado in our minds.

Many women lack the inner confidence necessary to make decisions that stick. Like a reed blowing in the wind, we bend this way and that when we are indecisive, which inevitably will break us. Confidence is the root that anchors us into the soil of self-awareness, making us steadfast and strong. When we are not confident with our decisions, the people around us sense that. We don't feel that we are worthy enough to make a decision to stand behind and that weakens our ability to lead effectively.

***Confidence is the root that anchors us into the soil of self-awareness, making us steadfast and strong.***

You rarely see men hemming and hawing over a decision in the workplace, or in life, for that matter. They generally think about it for a few minutes and then act. They make a decision and inform everyone that they have done so and what that decision entails. Even the manner in which they inform their employees is done with such conviction and steadfastness. There is no back and forth with men. Furthermore, very few men even have doubts about what they have decided when making a decision. They have such a strong sense of confidence when it comes to this, and it is innate.

Young boys, with few exceptions, are not taught or even subconsciously made to feel that they would not be able to achieve something or that they would have any limitations to the heights they wanted to soar. This confidence is so empowering, and to have it for the majority of your life engrains it in your DNA and it becomes a way of life for you.

We have all seen what confidence looks like in people—both men and women. It is so engaging and mesmerizing to watch them in action, isn't it? They almost saunter into a room, and they seem to have everything together and just go through the day making life-altering and financially staggering decisions in the blink of an eye. They clearly have the OM Factor. They truly flow and nothing gets in their way. That paralysis sometimes experienced by people who lack confidence never exists for them. They seem almost mythical.

The magnitude of the decision does not really come into play with them. This is key to their success. They take each decision and apply the same thought process to it without lacing it with fear and insecurity. When we entwine the decision with fear and insecurity, it not only clouds the decision that needs to be made, but it actually morphs the issue at hand into something that it really is not. It becomes this seemingly insurmountable mountain that in reality is a small hill. Certain decisions do require more time than others, but

***When we entwine the decision with fear and insecurity, it not only clouds the decision that needs to be made, but it actually morphs the issue at hand into something that it really is not.***

when you have inner confidence you are able to focus on the key factors and move forward.

This is very similar to the word problems that we had in school. Some people are completely thrown off when they see a word problem. There is something daunting about its appearance to some. If, when you look at a word problem and only see a bunch of words and feel intimidated by it, a relatively easy problem becomes much more challenging. However, when you look at the problem, cross out the parts that are superfluous and highlight the facts that are pertinent, you are only left with the meat on the bones and all the fat goes to the wayside. You can then tackle the problem and come up with a viable solution.

One reason that feeling a sense of confidence is challenging for some women is that we feel we will be completely defined by the choices we make. Some feel that advancing in the workplace is challenging enough and the margin for error for women is perceived to be significantly less. The inner terror that goes on inside leads us to lack confidence in our decisions as we feel that they may be the proverbial last words on our tombstones.

***One reason that feeling a sense of confidence is challenging for some women is that we feel we will be completely defined by the choices we make.***

This lack of confidence leads to indecisiveness. We feel that if we just took another few minutes or days or weeks to "think it through" we would have more security and perhaps make a better decision. Indecisiveness breeds chaos within the mind, thereby bringing out a tumultuous reality. When we are confident in our decisions we progress and create a reality that is evolutionary.

Do you think a caterpillar "thinks through" each of the steps it takes through its process of metamorphosis turning him into a beautiful butterfly? This amazing, life-altering process **just happens**. It happens because the caterpillar lets go. We need to let go. Let go of all the fear and insecurity and just take a decision with confidence and believe enough in ourselves that we too, will emerge into the beautiful butterfly.

## Taking to the Waters

Another soul-shifting experience for me was during an Aqua Zen treatment at Miraval. Here you are taken to a pool where there is only you and your therapist. The water at about 96 degrees is designed to be around the same as body temperature so that you are able to feel the sensation of the water as simply being an extension of your body. There is no beginning or end. It is simply just another part of you in a different medium. You are experiencing yourself both as a solid and a liquid at the same time. Although water comprises 70 percent of our bodies it is an invisible aspect of ourselves to us. This is why most of us, when we feel safe and secure, feel completely at home in the water.

You go into the waters and begin with your back against the wall with your therapist next to you. You are perfect strangers. The therapist asked me to gently close my eyes, and then a completely transformative experience took place. She asked me to lean my head back and I was literally floating in water while being cradled in the protective arms of my therapist. I was being totally nurtured. What a dichotomous experience—to be floating and still feel I would never, ever sink. She then said to me words that I have never heard before in my life: She said, "Don't worry. You can let go—I've got you." I cannot explain what those words both physically and mentally did for my being.

After an initial fleeting doubting feeling after hearing these foreign words, I completely succumbed. My shoulders loosened, my breath deepened and slowed down, and my entire being was light . . . free.

Our souls crave that. We want to feel protected and even "rescued" at times. This is a primal need and desire of women on a soul level. That feeling of complete blind trust is something many people are unable to experience after their childhood, and some of us not were not able even then. The sounds of your breath literally echo in your being. You hear your breath. You listen to it in a way that you are unable to while walking around or sitting normally outside of the water. It is the only sound you hear and resembles what we experience in the womb—the sound of the water displacing.

***We want to feel protected and even "rescued" at times. This is a primal need and desire of women on a soul level.***

It is as if you are so free that you would never come in harm's way. That knowingness is what we lack as humans. We lack this knowingness because life's experiences dictate otherwise. We enter this world completely dependent and completely open to trusting. As we grow up we realize we move towards having to be responsible for ourselves.

As time further passes we realize we are not only responsible for our own lives, but we must begin to be responsible for others as well. When this transition happens we sometimes lose sight of taking care of ourselves. Even on an airplane the attendant says, "In case of an emergency the oxygen masks will fall. Please put your oxygen mask on prior to assisting your child or others." This is counterintuitive for women. We would never think to do this as we are wired as nurturing beings. The challenge is that we don't realize that if we don't nurture ourselves we will be totally unable to take care of anyone else.

There is another component to this. We as women sometimes do not feel that we deserve to be taken care of and nurtured or deserve a sustained love. This comes down to a sense of self-worth that is not very strong in a lot of women. We feel that it is our duty to take care of home and family, but the theme of the conversation is rarely about what we need or what would make us feel whole and secure. Instead we feel divine order has been placed upon us, and we have been ordained to save the world, or if not the world, then at least everyone that crosses our path.

This sense of self is something that needs to be developed. You can get a very strong indication as to what your sense of self is by the answer to the question: Who am I? Most women will answer: I am a mother or I am a wife or I am a business owner, and so forth. None of these answers define or even remotely describe who we are as living, breathing, spiritual beings. These merely describe what role we have chosen to play in this lifetime. It does not describe our true essence. We feel much safer in this confined, organized, and accepted space. We feel we have some sort of sense of control and are accepted in society.

I mean, if you were to say to someone, "I am a spiritual being having a human experience" or "I am a loving, energetic being," you would probably have someone tilt their head and look at you like you have five noses or worse, politely nod and smile and their thought cloud is thinking that you are completely crazy. Our soul's imprint in it's manifestation is something much more multi-dimensional than what roles we take on in our life.

The kicker is that after all of this, the truth is that this sense of control that we have is truly a false sense. There is no control. There are merely choices that others make that when they are in agreement with our choice paradigms, make our ego feel that we have control. Our ego naively interprets the fact that if someone else may feel the way we do about something or just chooses to agree with us, that we have control over them. When you make a sales pitch to a client and they decide to buy whatever it is that you are selling, do they decide to do so because they were inclined to buy it in the first place or did you convince them?

We would like to think that we convinced the client, and we very well might have; however, that thought process comes from a very ego-based perspective. Chances are that they were inclined to buy the product or service, and our presentation or meeting solidified their desire to do so. If that is the case, then the false magnitude of the pitch need not plague us anymore.

***The truth is that this sense of control that we have is truly a false sense. There is no control. There are merely choices that others make that when they are in agreement with our choice paradigms, make our ego feel that we have control.***

Granted that our role is one that is necessary in closing the proverbial deal, everything does not hinge on it. Our role is to do our part, do it confidently, and let go of the outcome. When we have aligned our vibration with the other person by tailoring our communication to resonate with what they are interested in hearing and feeling at any given point in time, we will have done our part. The outcome will be a successful one as all of the energy in the room is focused on the same goal, and it's no longer about "having to make a sale," but rather "a conversation about collaboratively making things more efficient and effective."

## Rx to Heal Feelings of Indecisiveness

When feeling indecisive say the following affirmation quietly or silently:

*I am focused.*

OR

*OM Eim Saraswatayei Namaha*

The affirmation "I am focused" is very powerful because when we are focused and have "One-Pointedness" we have clarity as well as success. One-pointedness is a state of being completely focused or concentrating and being totally aware of and experiencing the present moment. When we repeat the affirmation "I am Focused" our thoughts start to rally around it and we begin to bring our attention to the present moment. All the other indecisive thoughts or chatter in our mind begin to slow down and eventually cease. Our tumultuous state of mind becomes uncluttered. This affirmation is beneficial because it also anchors us in the present moment where all things that we desire are manifested.

The mantra OM Eim Saraswatayei Namaha, (pronounced Aum I'm Sar-rah-swah-tee-yei Na-ma-ha), is a very powerful mantra and is believed to bring clarity and remove any obstacles that may arise within someone's career or education. This mantra invokes all of the traits of the Goddess Saraswati: knowledge, wisdom, memory, and creativity. I find this mantra to be extremely helpful in creating a strong sense of focus, decisiveness, and clarity when making any decisions in relation to a career and helping ignite creative discussion rather than mundane debate.

Every decision we make as leaders or within the workplace requires clarity as well as an open mind that is not clouded by the outside negative forces of fear and insecurity. When your mind is clear and open, many ideas come that would have never occurred to you initially. Also, this clarity of mind allows you to focus and make decisions in a more confident and steadfast manner.

Feeling indecisive can also really be helped by fostering and cultivating focus. This is so important that I wanted to give you another technique that you can do both in the moment or when you have more time and are alone as a meditation. This is called Kirtan Kriya or the SA TA NA MA meditation. This meditation focuses on chanting the sounds that signify the stages of life. Sa means birth, Ta means life, Na means death and Ma means rebirth. This meditation, that can be done in the moment when you are feeling indecisive or the need to feel more focused and centered, is extremely powerful and has many benefits that go beyond the balancing of the mind and bringing you to a more focused state.

This meditation helps to improve your memory and concentration, brings you to an emotionally balanced state, and reduces an inflammatory response in your body. Touching the different fingers stimulate different parts of your brain thereby regenerating it as well. This works by calming the nervous system and increasing blood flow to the memory structures of the brain.

This also increases the number of neurotransmitters that improve the communication between brain cells, thereby enhancing brain and memory function. There are many drugs that are prescribed to try to increase these transmitters, which are not always very effective, and this is a natural way to do this with wonderful results.

Harvard Medical School cited a study that was published in 2000 in the *Journal of Affective Disorders* where forty-five participants that were hospitalized for depression practiced Kirtan Kriya practiced for four weeks for thirty minutes a day, and 67 percent of the participants in the study achieved remission.

Patients with Alzheimer's disease also benefit when their caregivers practice this meditation. A study by the Alzheimer's Research and Prevention Foundation (ARPF) of depressed caregivers of family members with dementia, published in the *International Journal of Geriatric Psychiatry* online edition in March 2012, found that meditation increased telomerase, the enzyme that controls the length of your telomeres, which is the cap of your DNA. Longer telomeres mean a longer life and better health and shorter telomeres mean a shorter life, accelerated aging, and loss of cognitive functioning, including Alzheimer's disease.

In their study of highly stressed caregivers who did Kirtan Kriya for twelve minutes a day for eight weeks, an increase of 44 percent of telomerase was found, and this was the largest increase of telomerase ever seen. In this way meditation also may switch on your good genes and decrease the influence of your bad genes to improve memory.

I invite you to experience this profound meditation using the simple steps below. It has made a profound impact on me. I use it both as a cultivating practice in my morning meditation when I choose to take the twelve or so minutes to do it, and when I am in the moment at work or in a situation when I feel I need to get centered immediately and more focused.

### Kirtan Kriya: Sa Ta Na Ma Meditation

You may do this seated in a chair or sitting on the floor:

- Close your eyes to get focused for a few breaths
- Keep your hands on your knees and palms facing the ceiling
- Touch your index finger to your thumb while saying the sound "Saaa" aloud.
- Next, touch the tip of your middle finger with the tip of your thumb and say the sound "Taaa."
- Next, touch the tip of your ring finger with the tip of your thumb and say the sound "Naaa."
- Finally, touch the tip of your pinky with the tip of your thumb and say the sound "Maaa."

Continue the sequence of chanting Sa, Ta, Na, Ma for about two minutes aloud. Focus your attention in your third eye and visualize the sounds coming down from the universe through the crown of your head and out through your third eye. This is most commonly called the L form of concentration and is quite effective.

After chanting the sounds aloud for two minutes, move to whispering them for two minutes, and then silently in your mind saying them for four minutes. Then reverse the order and do whispering for two minutes and then finally aloud again for two minutes. Although this sequence takes about twelve minutes, do not focus on the time of how long you are doing each since that defeats the purpose. The key is to do it. You can also just do this aloud if you forget to go to the other stages of whispering and silence.

Also, if you are in the moment and need to do it then, feel free to do it any way that you can for as long as you are able. I have even had one or both of my hands under my desk while in a meeting and recited it in my mind silently. The SA TA NA MA is so powerful as it is a seed mantra that its effects are still there no matter how you do it.

You may also download a great App called "Stress Reduction Meditation: SA TA NA MA." It allows you to set the time and comes with voice and hand mudra instructions as well. The chimes then guide you through the practice. This is what you can use when you are doing it as part of your morning mediation and daily exercise of your brain.

When you finish inhaling and then exhale deeply, you can stretch your arms to the sky and bring them down again by your side.

*Kirtan Kriya Mudra Meditation*

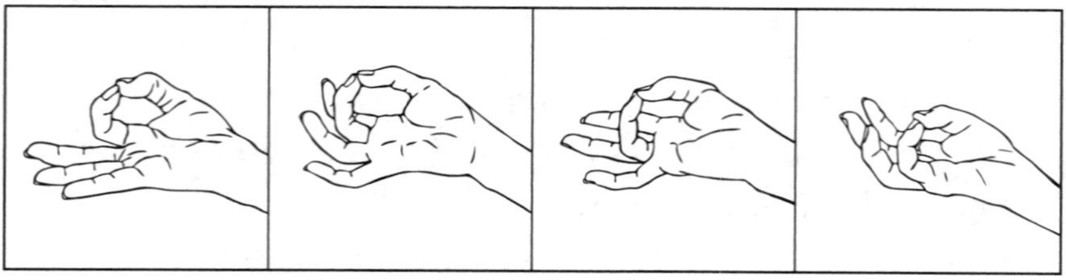

Saa Taa Maa Naa

### *Healing Gemstone: Garnet*

Garnet is the stone of passion and courage. Garnet focuses you on your purpose or goals. It increases your vitality and stamina. It is very good for career success, encouraging business relationships by increasing your popularity and stimulating other people's desire to work with you. It helps to become motivated and productive and attracts good luck in business ventures. The garnet is known as the stone for promoting a successful business. This stone enhances your charisma. It sparks creativity and can help get the creative juices flowing if they feel "blocked." You may put this stone in your purse, pocket and/or also have it on your desk in front of you to draw on its powerful properties.

*Immediate Steps to Take When Feeling Indecisive*

- Take a deep breath.
- Quietly or silently begin repeating the mantra or affirmation.
- Observe the change in yourself and the situation.

## 7 Daily Steps to Healing the Wound and Getting Your Two Extra Arms

1. Find a quiet place.
2. Close your eyes.
3. *Observe* your breath.
4. *Do not be judgmental if you have thoughts. Let them come and go.*
5. Repeat your mantra or affirmation if you wish, as if you are listening to it.
6. Picture what you are trying to manifest.
7. Let it go and continue steps 3-5 for whatever time you are able to sit.

# THE ROAD NOT TAKEN

*Two roads diverged in a yellow wood,*
*And sorry I could not travel both*
*And be one traveler, long I stood*
*And looked down one as far as I could*
*To where it bent in the undergrowth;*

*Then took the other, as just as fair,*
*And having perhaps the better claim*
*Because it was grassy and wanted wear,*
*Though as for that the passing there*
*Had worn them really about the same,*

*And both that morning equally lay*
*In leaves no step had trodden black.*
*Oh, I kept the first for another day!*
*Yet knowing how way leads on to way*
*I doubted if I should ever come back.*

*I shall be telling this with a sigh*
*Somewhere ages and ages hence:*
*Two roads diverged in a wood, and I,*
*I took the one less traveled by,*
*And that has made all the difference.*

—Robert Frost

## Tool 5

# WHEN YOU FEEL ANGER OR RESENTMENT

Letting go is vital for true transformation. Only once we let go can our reality change. How many times have we waited to hear the word "sorry" and held on to that which was serving us only to "be right"? Let me ask you—does that feeling of "being right" mean that much to you? Does it make you happy? Does it make you feel fulfilled? If you could just "be right" would all of your deepest desires be manifested for you to live the most glorious life you could imagine? I have learned (from Nelson Mandela) that holding onto something like this is like drinking poison and expecting the other person to die. That is just not smart, and it is frankly illogical. The only person that hurts and suffers from this is you.

We always wonder why the other person is not changing or why the situation or problem that we are facing is never solved. The reason we keep wondering this is because we are actually consciously set on holding on to this resentment and anger as if it is our security blanket. We feel deep down that if we forgive the person, we will then be vulnerable to this happening to us again, and we will be subjected to the unbearable pain yet again. Therein lies the fallacy of this thought process. When we forgive **we** are in control of how we feel about the person or situation after that. There is no more anger or resentment. There is only love.

> ***When we forgive we are in control of how we feel about the person or situation after that. There is no more anger or resentment. There is only love. Nothing will transform or change without letting go.***

Nothing will transform or change without letting go. Take a deep breath; now hold it, keep holding it, keep holding it . . . do you feel like you are going to suffocate and die? The answer is yes, and the ironic part of it is that ending that suffering and allowing that fresh new nourishing air to enter our body, that literally keeps us alive and thriving, requires us to just simply exhale. Yet we choose to feel that way and choose to continue to suffer knowing that it's in our control to end the suffering.

Anything, whether inanimate or animate, when pushed to a point beyond which it can sustain itself, will eventually cease to exist. A balloon, when filled with more air than it can contain, pops and can no longer be inflated. It's the same with human beings. The more we keep internalizing and holding onto that which does not serve us will only be detrimental to our existence.

When we let go of our memory of what happened that hurt us we can create a new memory in its place that is positive and brings us joy. That is also in our control. A memory is our recollection of an event or incident that happened. Generally the more traumatic or tragic the event is, the more vivid the memory is, and a lot of the time the more harmful. Conversely, the more joyful and happy the event is, the more blissful and nourishing the memory is.

We can actually manipulate our memories to bring joy and create new beginnings and a new life for ourselves. We cannot change what has happened. But we can change the way we remember what happened and the manner in which we perceive it. How would you like to remember that incident? What would you have done differently? What would you have said differently? Whom would you have reached out to and whom would you have forgiven?

If we close our eyes and remember the incident the way in which we would have liked it to have happened, we will realize that it is again all in our control. We can choose to hold on to being the victim or being the martyr or we can choose to be the hero and the protagonist in our own story as that is what a memory is—a story. It has already happened, so why would you continue to have it happen over and over again unless it is something that brings you joy?

## The Healing Technique of Holographic Memory Resolution (HMR®)

There is a patented technique called Holographic Memory Resolution (HMR®) developed by Dr. Brent Baum. Dr. Baum is a world-renowned therapist who has worked with the victims of the Oklahoma City bombing, 9/11, and a host of other tragedies as well as with people dealing with unpleasant events in life. HMR is a successful way to master the art of releasing and reframing a tragic or unpleasant incident in the past that is now a disturbing memory and replacing it with a pleasant one. This technique works by tapping into the subconscious mind to access the memory since our conscious minds rationalize too much. The best part is that many people experience positive results very quickly, often in the first session by not having to experience the painful experience of "reliving" past traumas.

Our conscious mind is our waking, breathing defense mechanism to protect us from what we perceive to be dangerous to our well-being. Our conscious minds assume that something that optically appears to be dangerous is truly dangerous. But things are not always what they seem.

When dealing with phobias or unpleasant experiences this is very effective. For example, let's say you are thirty years old and you have a very severe fear of heights. Every time you get near a ladder or a roller coaster your heart starts racing and you may even begin to perspire. There is no way that you will attempt to go on the roller coaster or climb the ladder. If anyone ever asked you why you were afraid of heights the chances are your response would be, "I don't know, I just am." Actually, it might turn out that there was an incident that happened when you were about eight years old that created an energetic imprint in your being. It was twenty-two years ago, and your conscious mind probably forgot about it or buried it. But the subconscious mind *never* forgets.

Perhaps when you were a child you were put on top of a refrigerator as a "game" with your siblings, and you were so high up that you couldn't get down and were paralyzed with fear. Since you didn't know when you were going to be taken down, you felt helpless, and your entire sense of physical and emotional security was robbed from you. You then buried this experience and moved through your journey of life seemingly unscathed. Unscathed, that is, until you found yourself in a trigger situation that began the domino effect of rapid heartbeat and perspiration along with a host of other physical symptoms.

A memory is actually a piece of the original experience. We actually re-experience the original experience the same way when the memory of it is triggered. Wouldn't it be great to reprogram that incident to something pleasant? If you could change the incident, what would you have liked to see happen? Perhaps you wouldn't have been placed on the refrigerator and would just be playing a simple game of hide and go seek with your siblings and everyone would be laughing and happy.

I was struggling with a mentally and emotionally debilitating tragedy that happened in my life. My best friend of twenty-three years, who was like a sister to me by any definition, was suddenly no longer in the manifested existence we know because of a tragic accident. I tried to make peace with it internally and let it go through all the methods that I knew how to utilize to help with this. I meditated as I did every day. I was confident that the practice that has been a true cure-all until that time in my life would definitely work. This didn't work because in meditation you are simply experiencing the beauty of the present moment. The simplicity of it. The breath flowing through the vessel of your stationary body. You are also letting go. I was now unable to do this. I felt deep inside that holding onto it would in some deranged way bring me closer to my dearest friend that I lost so tragically. I didn't want to let her go.

***A memory is actually a piece of the original experience. We actually re-experience the original experience the same way when the memory of it is triggered.***

I was so angry, devastated, and resentful that I was determined to not let the universe take that away from me as it did my friend. You see, holding on to things is truly a choice. We feel that it serves us. We won't admit it out loud to anyone as it is irrational. By doing this, we are basically saying: I choose to be miserable and I like it that way. I want to be unhappy, and peace is something that doesn't really appeal to me.

I tried hypnosis, thinking that if I was in an altered state of mind that my subconscious could help me rationalize and hopefully eradicate the incident completely from my mind. That didn't work because I was running away and not confronting it.

Then, the stars aligned at the time they were supposed to and my path crossed with Dr. Brent Baum. I was fortunate to be able to have a couple of one-on-one sessions with Dr. Baum and was able to experience the shift myself. By pinpointing where in your body you are holding the memory of the experience and the negative feeling and by sensing the size, shape, and color of it you can actually eradicate the negativity and replace the negative memory of the experience with a very positive one.

You do this by experiencing the negative memory real time and truly analyzing it. In this way you are freed from the obsessive focus on the terrible event or a phobia to replace the event with a positive memory—for instance, with an image of a wonderful memory of a person before his or her tragic death when you were happy together.

In life, half of what makes something scary or causes us to be fearful of something is the unknown nature of it. Our imagination and subconscious get together over cocktails and create a reality that is far more frightening and daunting than the actual events that took place. There is no doubt that a tragic event, or a phobia, or an unpleasant event of any sort is awful when it happens. However, we have the ability to heal through the replacing of the negative memory with a positive one. Nothing can change what happened, but how we perceive it, and how we heal from it, can.

When we experience an event there is also an element of surprise as we are in the present moment going through it. We are not doing Monday morning quarterbacking at the time we are experiencing something. So, we don't have the benefit or even the awareness at that moment of analyzing why we are reacting the way that we are to a particular situation or towards a particular person.

The beauty of HMR® is that you are able to take a very proactive approach to not only understanding why you may be feeling anger or resentment or other negative feelings, but also doing something about it by replacing it with a more pleasant memory or perhaps a way you would have liked things to be. This technique can work with debilitating fears, confrontational interactions in life or at work, tragic life events, or even conflicts within yourself that you are struggling with. I encourage you to research this technique further or find a therapist in your area that specializes in this technique if this resonates with you.

You are no longer a prisoner of your own self-destructive memories and feelings about a certain event or person. Imagine that you can navigate through your life as the true captain of your ship. That is incredibly liberating.

*Change your reality. Rewrite your story.*

*Choose life, choose love, choose happiness.*

## Rx to Heal Feelings of Anger and Resentment

When feeling anger or resentment say the following affirmation quietly or silently:

*I forgive everyone including myself.*

OR

*Om Tare Tuttare Ture Svaha*

As in the prayer of Saint Francis "Where there is injury, let me bring pardon." The teaching is to bring love to hate, light to darkness, and pardon to injury. Being mindful of these three acts, you realize that you have the power to do all of these things. When you can bring love to where there was once hate, illuminate the depths of where there was once darkness, and forgive someone or even yourself from injury—whether it is inflicted or self-inflicted—there is nothing that can impede pure joy in your life.

The affirmation "I forgive everyone including myself" is so powerful because most of the time we interpret forgiveness to be an external act. That only solves half of the equation. Even if you are not the one who may have inflicted the initial injury, you have contributed to it by internalizing the pain and harboring anger and resentment about it. Resentment and anger can only thrive in an environment of hatred and stubbornness. That is an internal choice. In order to solve the equation you must, as in algebra, make sure

***Resentment and anger can only thrive in an environment of hatred and stubbornness. That is an internal choice.***

both sides are equal. That means forgiving others as well as yourself. The result is always love.

The mantra "OM Tare Tuttare Ture Svaha," pronounced (Aum Taa-re Too-tare Too-rey Sva-ha), is the mantra of liberation. It is liberation from Samsara, which is the wheel of life—liberation from suffering, guilt, anger, and resentment, and it is the mantra to bring forgiveness into the fold. The meaning of the mantra is broken down in the following manner: *OM Tara* invokes compassion into our beings; *Tuttare* liberates us from the delusions that cause suffering; *Ture* liberates us from the perception of duality. To believe that suffering is solely of the self is a misconception. To practice true compassion one must link personal suffering to the suffering of others; *Svaha* is the final syllable that cements the meaning of the mantra in your consciousness.

This mantra is most closely associated with the heart chakra, which is the fourth chakra. This is the chakra of forgiveness, unconditional love, letting go, trust, and compassion. You may do this mantra with the mala when you do your meditation and you can also use it when you are in an acute situation where you feel anger or resentment and want to replace it with feelings of forgiveness and compassion. This powerful mantra enables your heart chakra to open like a lotus flower and radiate vibrations of loving kindness and compassion to all sentient beings and most especially to yourself.

### *Healing Gemstone: Sugalite*

Sugalite is a sometimes known as the "healer's stone." It can draw out inflammation, stress, and emotional blockages. It absorbs and dissolves anger. You can use this stone to lower your anger, jealousy, and resentment. You may put this stone in your purse, pocket, and/ or also have it on your desk in front of you to draw on its powerful properties.

*Immediate Steps to Take When Feeling Anger or Resentment*

- Take a deep breath.
- Quietly or silently begin repeating the mantra or affirmation.
- Observe the change in yourself and the situation.

## 7 Daily Steps to Healing the Wound and Getting Your Two Extra Arms

1. Find a quiet place.
2. Close your eyes.
3. *Observe* your breath.
4. *Do not be judgmental if you have thoughts. Let them come and go.*
5. Repeat your mantra or affirmation if you wish, as if you are listening to it.
6. Picture what you are trying to manifest.
7. Let it go and continue steps 3-5 for whatever time you are able to sit.

# ALL THAT WE ARE

*All that we are is the result of what we have thought:*
*It is founded on our thoughts,*
*It is made up of our thoughts.*
*If a man speaks or acts with an evil thoughts,*
*Pain follows him as the wheel follows*
*The foot of the ox that draws the carriage.*
*All that we are is the result of what we have thought:*
*It is founded on our thoughts,*
*It is made up of our thoughts.*
*If a man speaks or acts with a pure thought,*
*Happiness follows him*
*Like a shadow that never leaves him.*
*"He abused me, he beat me,*
*He defeated me, he robbed me,"–*
*In those who harbor such thoughts*
*Hatred will never cease*
*"He abused me, he beat me,*
*He defeated me, he robbed me,"–*
*In those who do not harbor such thoughts*
*Hatred will cease.*
*For hatred does not cease by hatred at any time;*
*Hatred ceases by love; this is an old rule.*

—DHAMMAPADA

# Tool 6

# WHEN YOU FEEL TAKEN ADVANTAGE OF

Picture this familiar scene: Your desk is so buried in sticky notes that your workspace looks as though it has been professionally wallpapered. Your phone light is perpetually on, and the display shows ten voicemails that have not been listened to because you are answering dozens of emails that request an immediate response. While your desk is piled with papers a foot high, the folder for completed projects remains empty as you try to tackle the seemingly self-replicating and infinitely present paper-stack. Everything on the sticky notes has the words URGENT, STAT, or ACTION written on them, and you feel like you are an emergency room doctor instead of a corporate worker bee.

You lift your gaze from the glaring computer screen to which your eyes are affixed for the majority of the time as you see someone hovering at your cubicle or office door through your peripheral vision—and this is when it happens. You hear the words, "I know you are so busy, but could you please give your comments on this and handle the rest of this PowerPoint presentation—it is URGENT."

Through the other corner of your eye you can feel the sticky notes and emails converging to form a huge Jabba The Hut glob that is inching its way towards you. You say, "Sure, just put it in my inbox."

Whether it is in the office or at home, women do not naturally feel comfortable saying "no." It is a learned word for us. The interesting thing is that even when we have learned that it is okay to say no, we tend to act like martyrs and take it all on. Why does this happen? Why do we do this? Personal boundaries—or rather, lack thereof.

The definition of boundary is "a line that marks the limit of an area; a dividing line." There are two key words here that elicit a visceral response from women: limits and dividing. We don't like to set limits and we certainly do not like to divide; we like to unite. Most women are not taught from an early age how to establish personal boundaries. We are taught to manage and excel at everything. We are taught that we are the glue that holds the family together. We are taught that in order to move up the corporate ladder and not bang our head on the glass ceiling we need to distinguish ourselves and be able to handle everything and not be the one to say that we need to take our child to soccer practice and can therefore not attend that meeting. That is a lot of pressure that is actually self-imposed. (I know . . . I know . . . hear me out on this one. Keep reading).

***Whether it is in the office or at home, women do not naturally feel comfortable saying "no." It is a learned word for us. The interesting thing is that even when we have learned that it is okay to say no, we tend to act like martyrs and take it all on.***

What we need to realize is that we are doing this to ourselves. So what if we are not taught this. We know now that although diamonds are made from intense pressure at very high temperatures they are inherently flawed. They look beautiful on the outside and their flaws can be masked by their color (makeup) or cut (physical appearance), but the true clarity of the diamond when viewed under the loop is something that cannot be masked. Inclusions that are not visible to the naked eye are then exposed and one either decides that superficial color and cut are more important and accepts this, or goes deeply within and realizes that clarity is the true essence. As Daniel Defoe profoundly said, "The soul is placed in the body like a rough diamond, and must be polished, or the luster of it will never appear." This means no matter how much makeup you use or how much physical exercise you do, unless you strengthen your inner self—your soul—your true essence and beauty will never be exposed.

***The true clarity of the diamond when viewed under the loop is something that cannot be masked. Inclusions that are not visible to the naked eye are then exposed and one either decides that superficial color and cut are more important and accepts this, or goes deeply within and realizes that clarity is the true essence.***

By establishing definite personal boundaries you won't feel that self-deprecating sense of being taken advantage of because you will be so *clear* inside at the level of the soul. You will not have that inner quandary of "Should I take this on or not" or "What will they think if I say no. Will they perceive me as weak?" You will be crystal *clear* as to what is acceptable, safe, reasonable, and permissible for you because you will have established it yourself. Fluid boundaries create nothing but confusion and chaos for everyone involved.

There are no cookie-cutter answers here. The parameters are different for everyone as each person has her or his own inner makeup and design. What works for one person may not work for someone else. We are all on our own individual journeys through life, and the road map is not a one-size-fits-all type of thing.

You will find your own personal boundaries when you go within yourself during your time of meditation, as you will be able to attune yourself to spirit, and it will let you know by what feels right or wrong for you. When you work on building your OM Factor during these times, you will know the answers real-time since you will be completely in tune with yourself. Then even when you set limits or dividing lines they will no longer feel like you are doing something wrong; they will feel infinitely right.

## Communicating with Others in a Healthy Manner

OK. Now we have established how to develop our own personal healthy boundaries, but how do we convey what they are to others? Most human beings are not mind readers, and because people operate under their own rules and paradigms they probably would not have gotten the memo that they crossed a personal boundary. Women struggle with how they convey what their personal boundaries are without, and here's the key, "offending" anyone. We are so afraid of offending someone, thinking we may be passed up for a promotion from their thinking less of us, or perhaps even getting fired, that we sometimes suffer silently and do not speak up.

***Women struggle with how they convey what their personal boundaries are without, and here's the key, "offending" anyone.***

It is OK to speak up. It does not have to be done in a firing-line sort of way where you bombard people. Standing up for yourself is not something that should be frowned upon, and most of the time what we don't realize is that people end up respecting us more when we stand up for ourselves—as long as it's done in a productive, healthy, and kind manner.

You simply need to say that you are unable to comply with the request at this time as you have other things that need your undivided attention at this moment and must take priority. You can follow that statement with "When I am able to make your request a priority, which it deserves, I would be more than happy to, but at this time I am unfortunately unable." The second statement should only be said if you truly feel that way. There is no need to go beyond the first statement if you feel uncomfortable.

If the person insists, for example in the workplace, that their task takes priority, you need to inform them that you will have no problem making it a priority, but something else that has been tasked to do before this must be lowered in priority.

No one will benefit from a hodge-podge job done on a project or tasks that are not fully completed to the best of your ability. When this is conveyed in a rational manner during a discussion, the result is a favorable one for all parties. The challenge only arises when the fear of a negative reaction overpowers us and renders us mute in communicating. When we don't communicate, we cannot then expect the other person to understand. The fear needs to be replaced by a sense of empowerment that comes from making the conscious choice of setting these personal boundaries and communicating them in a healthy manner.

***The fear needs to be replaced by a sense of empowerment that comes from making the conscious choice of setting these personal boundaries and communicating them in a healthy manner.***

This method can also be translated into any interaction. Be clear about what your boundaries are, and then be confident in letting others know when they may have inadvertently or sometimes intentionally crossed the line. Why is it that computers, non-human objects, never cross boundaries? Because the person who wrote the code put in "if/then" statements to only allow certain levels of access or certain outputs. They are set up to only allow certain individuals to access them at certain levels depending on the priority. We take the time to do this with computers, but we do not do it with one another as human beings. Let us take the time and write our own personal inner code and follow that.

A very interesting study conducted by the Families and Work Institute, Catalyst, and Boston College Center for Work and Family from 2000–2003, illustrates this. The study is called "Leaders in a Global Economy." The study took a group of executives and asked them a series of questions on balancing work and family life. In this study balance did not necessarily mean that in order to achieve one thing that you had to give up something else; it did not mean that to be successful at work you needed to "give up" some aspects of your personal/family life. This study found the exact opposite to be true. The study found several important things.

- People who had jobs that fulfilled them and had supportive work environments were much more likely to be in better moods and happier, and therefore were more likely and able to impart that happiness to their families or loved ones at home.
- Achieving the balance of work and personal life is based on how people determine and set their priorities.
- 61 percent of the group turned out to be "work centric" which was not so surprising. These people put their work before their jobs.
- 32 percent put the *same* priority on their jobs in the workplace and also their personal lives outside the workplace. They called these people "dual centric people." These people felt successful at work and were much less stressed. These people set very strict boundaries and when they were engaged with people or in a task they were present. They were emotionally and physically present.

It brings us back to the simple fact of the importance of taking time to nurture ourselves and that by doing this we nurture all of our interactions in the process. Establishing healthy boundaries allows us to feel empowered and fulfilled, and that translates into a domino effect to all aspects of our lives. When we view ourselves as multi-dimensional beings and adopt a holistic 360 degree view of ourselves rather than a two-dimensional one, we will make all aspects of ourselves a priority. We do this because when we see all aspects of our lives (work, family, community, personal relationships) as important and a priority, a balance naturally emerges.

## Rx to Heal Feelings of Being Taken Advantage Of

When feeling taken advantage of say the following affirmation quietly or silently:

*I am Balanced.*

OR

*Shiva Shakti*

The affirmation "I am Balanced" immediately gives our minds a visual of brass scales in equilibrium. It gives both a relaxing as well as comforting feeling throughout our bodies. You immediately breathe deeper and exhale. You may picture yourself doing yoga, or enjoying a refreshing beach breeze as it grazes over your face, or the loving faces of those dear to you. You feel as if anything is possible and you can move on with your tasks at hand with ease and with a smile. Nothing seems to be exasperating, everything is prioritized, and you are fully present. Repeating this in the moment brings everything back to a Zen-like state and you are empowered with your own priorities and boundaries that you have taken the time to create.

The mantra "Shiva Shakti" (pronounced Shi-vah Shuk-thi) is extremely powerful and empowering. It embraces both the masculine and the physical aspects of our being. We take on a holistic, 360 degree view of ourselves and the energetic power that we harness by embracing both aspects in a balanced state of mind. Shiva (masculine) is recognized as the embodiment of pure consciousness and Shakti (feminine) is the embodiment of pure energy. Your inner Shakti is the essence of feminine life force energy. From this essence you experience beauty, creativity, power, ability, and playful energy. Shakti is known as the mother of creation and manifests in many forms. Your inner Shiva is your embodiment of awareness and consciousness. This is the awareness that is ever present and witnesses all experiences and embraces life as an expression of the divine.

Shiva is the masculine energy that represents transcendence, liberation, and bliss. When our inner Shiva and Shakti are in balance the result is pure happiness and bliss. We are able to flow with whatever comes our way and have clarity. Through this union comes harmony in all aspects of our life. Just as Shiva and Shakti are both parts of the whole of our being, making sure that we honor and nurture all aspects of ourselves is key to feeling fulfilled and whole. Repeating this mantra during times of feeling taken advantage of will bring about a sense of empowerment and balance to your being.

### *Healing Gemstone: Agate*

Agate is a very powerful stone that is ideal in these situations. Agate fosters feelings of acceptance, balance, harmony, peace, and appreciation. Agate is an ideal stone for situations that are stressful or those that demand great courage. Agate is a stone of strength. Agate can also generate a sense of love, protection, security, luck, and abundance. It also has very harmonious qualities where it can improve relationships and release feelings of resentment.

Whenever you feel being taken advantage of, hold the Agate in your hand and hold it up to your heart center for a few minutes and you will feel the feeling of disempowerment slowly going away and replacing itself with a strong sense of empowerment. You can keep this in your purse or on your desk at work.

### *Immediate Steps to Take When Feeling Taken Advantage Of*

- Take a deep breath.
- Quietly or silently begin repeating the mantra or affirmation.
- Observe the change in yourself and the situation.

## 7 Daily Steps to Healing the Wound

1. Find a quiet place.
2. Close your eyes.
3. *Observe* your breath.
4. *Do not be judgmental if you have thoughts. Let them come and go.*
5. Repeat your mantra or affirmation if you wish, as if you are listening to it.
6. Picture what you are trying to manifest.
7. Let it go and continue steps 3-5 for whatever time you are able to sit.

# YOU ARE THE INFINITE SPIRIT

*All these small ideas that*
*I am a man or a woman,*
*Sick or healthy, strong or weak,*
*Or that I hate or love or have little power,*
*are but hallucinations.*

*Stand up then!*
*Know that every thought and word*
*That weakens you in this world is the only evil that exists.*
*Stand as a rock; you are the Infinite Spirit.*
*Say, "I am Existence Absolute,*
*Bliss Absolute, Knowledge Absolute,"*
*and like a lion breaking its cage,*
*break your chains and be free forever.*

*What frightens you, what holds you down:*
*Only ignorance of your true nature,*
*of your blessedness; nothing else can bind you.*
*You are the Pure one, the Ever-Blessed.*

*Therefore, if you dare, stand on that—*
*mold your whole life on that.*
*You are the one with the Eternal Soul.*
*Know then that thou art He,*
*and model your whole life accordingly;*
*for those who know this*
*and model their lives accordingly,*
*will no more suffer in darkness.*

—Swami Vivekananda

## Tool 7

# WHEN YOU FEEL DISRESPECTED

A wise person once told me, "What other people think of you is none of your business." I replayed that statement in my head over and over again when I heard it so that I could really *hear* it. At first, I thought, "that's true" and went about my business. Then I thought, "Wait a minute . . . that is really true." I realized one important thing that I think I was missing for a very long time. A light bulb went off inside me. It was in *MY* control—my own personal control as to whether or not I felt disrespected or slighted. Someone could tell me I was not good enough, overweight, talk over me in a meeting—or worse, nod politely in a meeting, smile and say thanks, and then turn her or his head to a trusted advisor for the input that they were looking for.

In all of those examples one would feel diminished or disrespected at first. You think "why am I being so disrespected?" "Why is he or she talking to me in that manner?" The question should be "Why am I allowing myself to be so disrespected?" "Why am I allowing this to consume me?"

However, if you take a moment and reframe it in your mind immediately—and I mean immediately—your mind will not even go in that direction. Reframe it in your mind and realize that those are only words that they are saying, and it is you that attach meaning to them. Positive or negative. Simply do not allow it to be anything other than productive. You will find yourself actually smiling and feeling pity for the other person initially. That is not the best thing either, but try it. It actually works!

That said, you want to get to a point where you smile and feel a sense of understanding that they are just operating at their own vibration and level of consciousness, and that these are their own personal feelings and really have nothing at all to do with you whatsoever. That is really empowering, isn't it?

Disrespectful behavior in the workplace runs rampant and is sometimes shown as very subtle hostility, and other times it is blatant. This is nothing short of bullying, and it is on the rise. The National Institute for Occupational Safety and Health when researching stress in the workplace in 2004 found that 24.5 percent of companies surveyed reported instances of bullying. This leads to many negative things that compromise the health of the company and of the employees. When employees ignore and disregard the opinions of their coworkers, those on the receiving end of the disrespect get very defensive. Lack of trust and a feeling of being violated then emerge, and this compromises any sense of teamwork.

Teams must perform at a very high level to be successful, and this erodes their ability to do so. In a situation like this there is also very high turnover. People feel that higher salaries and perks are not worth the stress of being disrespected. They would rather earn a bit less and feel valued as employees than subject themselves day in and day out to that.

Because of this decrease in productivity and increase in personnel turnover there is a definite impact on profits. Most of the time is spent on diffusing or engaging in conflicts. This disrespect can show itself in many different forms. It can range from people ignoring meetings, sending offensive emails or texts, surfing the Internet, or just staying at home, as they would rather do that then come into work. The company's financial health is definitely affected.

The challenge comes when we allow other's negative opinions of ourselves, whether it is about our appearance, positions at work, level of education, our character, or even the way we speak, to mold us and become our new beings. In our own minds we literally morph into the way others view us and also manifest that. Our shoulders begin to slump, we may cry a lot, get physically ill from digestive issues and lack of sleep, and suffer from depression. It is kryptonite-like and weakens our inner source. We actually become all of their stuff that they thrust upon us and accept it as if there is no other choice.

Remember that bullies are cowards and get their fuel from very deep-seated insecurities and fears. Those are their personal issues, not yours.

This concept of morphing into someone or something else was illustrated vividly while I was reading a very disturbing story the other day. A drug dealer had housed a lion, a tiger, and a bear since they were cubs. He did not properly care for them. The bear's harness grew into his skin because the owner did not adjust it as the animal grew. The animals that were abused as they grew were thankfully finally rescued.

Aside from the obvious cruelty, there was something that really struck me. The bear's harness had *grown* into his skin. It became part of his being. The neglect and abuse infused themselves into his soul and became a part of him. This was so much so that they had to surgically remove the harness when he was rescued.

As human beings, we cannot have this trauma and abuse surgically removed from us. At best, we pay for some expensive therapy and hope to miraculously be cured or at least be able to function in society without walking around with that sinking feeling inside or admitted in a hospital for physical or mental ailments. Normally, unfortunately, we just go through life accepting this disrespect and it makes 1,000 small cuts in our soul. That is torture. It is those little cuts that chip away at you and your self-esteem. They may not bleed profusely at the onset, but at the end they most certainly kill you.

***As human beings, we cannot have this trauma and abuse surgically removed from us. At best, we pay for some expensive therapy and hope to miraculously be cured or at least be able to function in society without walking around with that sinking feeling inside or admitted in a hospital for physical or mental ailments.***

Because the blood does not gush from these cuts as it would from a gunshot wound, sometimes people around us that care for us deeply cannot even see the wounds that we are carrying.

We walk around with a physical smile on our faces, and all the while our hearts are crying the tears of a thousand oceans. Why do we do this? Why do we allow this? We do this because deep down we do not have the self-confidence and self-love that is required to fight against these outside forces. This is something that takes work and needs to be built over time.

## Creating a Shield of Armor from Within

We must create a shield of armor around ourselves in order to protect ourselves from these attacks. This shield that is self-created comes from deep within our souls through connecting with our source in moments of silence. When we go within during silence we hear the heartbeat of our inner desires and feel peace. No one can control that or take that away from us. This is something that is cultivated. If you are lucky, it is cultivated when you are very young by your parents and family around you who build you up and increase your self-confidence and self-love.

For those that are not as lucky, you can absolutely cultivate this shield yourself. The beauty of the energy of this shield is that it is composed of such a pure, vibrant, and, most importantly, an infinite energy that is omnipresent and omnipotent.

This energy is the energy of love. Love has no beginning and no end. It has no judgment. Love is pure, fulfilling, and extremely powerful. It can annihilate hate, violence, and abuse. We have experienced this feeling when we look into the eyes of our children, pets, or people that we feel a deep affection for. You feel as though you are in paradise. Nothing else matters at that moment when you experience the feeling of love. It transcends all of the external drama and engulfs you in a cocoon of warmth, comfort, and safety. It is available to anyone who desires to tap into it.

The only reason love seems elusive to us at times is that we are so consumed with the negativity around us and the events that are unfolding negatively, that we are blinded by them. We let the events overpower us and become our reality. This is most certainly a choice and one that will always keep love hidden from our sight.

***The only reason love seems elusive to us at times is that we are so consumed with the negativity around us and the events that are unfolding negatively, that we are blinded by them. We let the events overpower us and become our reality.***

In order to accomplish this you have to do only one thing: love yourself unconditionally. Love every aspect of yourself unconditionally, including your perceived flaws and strengths and your imperfections and your beauty. Everything must be embraced equally. When we embrace every aspect of ourselves we realize we are not a sum of parts, good and bad. There is no longer a good and bad.

This is a very important shift that absolutely must happen in your mind in order for it to translate in your soul. *It is all the same.* You are no longer defined as a good person or a bad person. No one person is all good or all bad. We simply have different aspects of ourselves that make up who we are. We must accept all of these sides of ourselves in order to evolve. When we truly accept ourselves we don't bother about trivial subtleties and perceived imperfections. When we accept ourselves, we are vibrating with the heartbeat of the soul, which is love.

So, love yourself unconditionally and you will never ever feel that you are defined by someone else's paradigms. Nor will anyone else's opinion of you ever bother you or make you feel diminished or disrespected. You will simply feel love and radiate love.

## Rx to Heal Feelings of Disrespect

When feeling disrespect say the following affirmation quietly or silently:

*I am worthy.*

OR

*Ham Sah*

To feel worthy is to feel whole. To feel worthy is to feel that you deserve respect, love, and equanimity. This affirmation very swiftly aligns your mind with your heart. Your mind hears the words and processes them and your heart feels them and feels a sense of belonging and peace. You are immediately transported from a state of feeling "less than" to being empowered and whole. There is nothing more empowering than to feel that you deserve a seat at the table and you are claiming that seat. Disrespect no longer has a place in your universe and vanishes.

The mantra "Ham-Sah" (pronounced, "hum-saa), translates to "I AM THAT." This is the essence of our beings. We are that. Good,

Bad, Light, and Darkness. That which you think someone else is, you are, and that which you are makes up someone else. It is said that this mantra helps us to erase the sense of duality and the feeling that we are separate from the other. There are blurred lines that emerge where you drew them in the sand. You completely and utterly accept all of yourself, and the shield of love envelopes you and you are embraced and protected.

On average, 21,600 times during the day we actually chant this mantra. "Ha" is the sound of the breath on our exhalation and "Sa" is the sound of the inhalation. The "m" sound between the ha and the sa represents the individual who is the focal point of energy and intelligence. When you close your eyes and repeat this mantra you will start to feel the energy moving within you. It is immediate. You can also repeat this with your eyes open. This is a very empowering and energizing mantra and rescues you from any self-depreciating feelings or fears with every exhalation.

### *Healing Gemstone: Tigers Eye*

Tiger's eye is a beautiful stone that combines the grounding energy of the earth with the uplifting energy of the sun. It helps you face and overcome challenges. It helps you recognize your own needs and be true to them. It imbues us with willpower, purpose, courage, and self-confidence. It is also a very protective stone and should be taken during your travels as well. Many people wear this in the form of a beaded bracelet for constant protection from that which does not serve them. You may put this stone in your purse, pocket, and/or also have it on your desk in front of you to draw on its powerful properties. Many people even wear bracelets of tiger's eye beads as a constant protection.

*Immediate Steps to Take When Feeling Disrespected*

- Take a deep breath.
- Quietly or silently begin repeating the mantra or affirmation.
- Observe the change in yourself and the situation.

## 7 Daily Steps to Healing the Wound and Getting Your Two Extra Arms

1. Find a quiet place.
2. Close your eyes.
3. *Observe* your breath.
4. *Do not be judgmental if you have thoughts. Let them come and go.*
5. Repeat your mantra or affirmation if you wish, as if you are listening to it
6. Picture what you are trying to manifest.
7. Let it go, and continue steps 3-5 for whatever time you are able to sit.

# THE SHORELESS OCEAN

*In me the limitless ocean,*
*on the rising of the wind of the mind,*
*diverse waves of worlds are produced.*
*With the calming of the wind of the mind,*
*In the infinite ocean of myself,*
*The seemingly self vanishes*
*How wonderful!*
*In me, the shoreless ocean,*
*the waves of individual selves,*
*according to their nature,*
*rise, strike each other,*
*play for a time, and then disappear.*

—Astavakra Samhita

## Part III

# BUILDING YOUR OM FACTOR FOR LIFE:

## *Traits to Cultivate for Extraordinary Results*

## Trait 1

# BE PRESENT

Many times we are so busy wondering about what happened yesterday or five minutes ago, or what will happen tomorrow or five minutes from now, that what we are actually thinking about has either already happened or might never happen. What is actually occurring becomes the past since we weren't there for it. The present moment vanishes. No intention is set, let alone realized. We then wallow in our life wondering why things aren't changing and why we are in the same rut. A well-known definition of insanity is "making the same mistakes over and over again and expecting a different result."

There is no arguing the fact that practicing living in the present is challenging to do when you attempt to put it into practice. It is a challenge only because we are trained as humans to "plan for the future." We are not taught or trained to live in the present moment. Everything we are taught hovers around the idea that scarcity is imminent, and one must plan to overcome and hopefully avoid this. Planning is surely vital to survival and success; however it should certainly not be at the expense of leaving the fertile ground of creativity barren.

Creativity solely functions in the present moment and its engine is only fueled by the awareness of one's personal footprint. If you notice, when you have an aha moment or a moment when you feel like you have an idea, it seems to come out of nowhere, doesn't it?

You are not sitting banging your head saying "I need an idea . . . I need an idea." Surely, if you do that nothing will come. You will be sitting at your office desk, working on a project, and all of a sudden you will have an amazing idea come to you that you weren't expecting. You may be in the shower, and while the water is cascading down your body and you are passively listening to it beat against the tiles below your feet, you figure out the solution to a problem that has been plaguing you. It comes out of nowhere—or so it seems.

***Creativity solely functions in the present moment and its engine is only fueled by the awareness of one's personal footprint.***

Actually, the idea is much more calculated and orchestrated than it seems at first glance. It all starts with you planting a seed. This seed may not initially be planted intentionally, but it is planted nonetheless. This is the seed of intention. It is planted in the fertile ground of creativity and what manifests is your deepest desire. Your heart plants this intention, not your mind. This intention is not something that you sit and think about logically by using your mind.

This intention is something that you feel in your heart. It is your deepest desire. It may be specific or vague, material, or ethereal. Maybe it's to be the most successful executive in your firm, own your own business, or make a difference in a person's life through philanthropy. Once that seed is planted, the universe conspires to fulfill this desire by aligning the series of events that need to occur in order for this desire to be manifested.

***There are no coincidences. No one crosses your path by accident. There are only moments where opportunity and timing intersect and you are at the proverbial "right place at the right time."***

There are no coincidences. No one crosses your path by accident. There are only moments where opportunity and timing intersect and you are at the proverbial "right place at the right time." You feel inside that things are going smoothly and somehow things work out. People use the term "the stars aligned." This is not far from the truth. Many things need to take place to pave the way of your path to get to your goal.

## Awareness, Mindfulness, and Intuition

As you are reading this, you are probably thinking back to something that happened in your life that was impactful and was something you really wanted. Think about how you achieved it. Really think about it. You will then notice that you probably met someone along the way that was influential in making an introduction or someone that inspired you to take a particular step in a direction that you otherwise wouldn't have gone. When you have the awareness that it is beyond your own efforts and your ego takes a bit of a back seat, you realize that it's bigger than you.

Being in the present moment is a practice. It is something that you need to be consciously very aware of and practice it as you would any type of sport or skill. If you take the time to understand why it is completely life changing by putting you at the helm of your own ship rather than being a passenger, you begin to see the power of this essential practice.

The beauty of this practice is that you can do it at any given moment. There does not have to be the "right" atmosphere, you can be in a huge crowd or can be in the shower. The only thing that you need is to be mindful and aware that you are a living, breathing being that is powerful and can influence the fulfillment of your deepest desires.

When you are mindful and aware of what you are experiencing at any given moment you are open to infinite possibilities without judgment. You notice the events unfolding around you as well as the emotions ebbing and flowing within you. When you "notice" and don't "judge," you are in the present moment. Emotions don't take a life of their own; they are simply feelings that you are experiencing. They come and they go. They are not permanent, just as you experience the events that unfold. You notice that you may be feeling scared, angry, sad, or happy. You notice that the man sitting at the table next to you is wearing a black jacket and blue jeans. These are things that are happening NOW. Most of the time, unfortunately, we are ever present in worrying about what will happen or what did happen that we completely miss what *is* happening.

***When you "notice" and don't "judge," you are in the present moment. Emotions don't take a life of their own; they are simply feelings that you are experiencing. They come and they go. They are not permanent, just as you experience the events that unfold.***

This practice cultivates that awareness and mindfulness and brings us in the present moment immediately. A simple trick is to tell yourself to inhale and exhale. You are immediately present and in one fell swoop connected to your breath, mind, and body. Now, look around you—things look different than they did five minutes ago, don't they? They appear different because you are different. You are more aware and you are officially in the present moment.

Another great benefit that being present provides is that it opens us up to intuition. Intuition is that little voice inside that tells us to watch out or forge ahead with abandon. We all have this voice. Some of us pay attention to it and some of us don't. We must listen to our inner voices and being present helps us to tune into it more clearly. This voice is one that you always refer to when you are doing your Monday morning quarterbacking and say, "I should have listened to you." When you practice being present you will notice this voice getting louder and more frequent. You will also notice that those seemingly infrequent coincidences will start to become more frequent and you will be in awe of the sight before you.

Those who have The OM Factor have cultivated their intuition to such a level through the practice of being present, that this becomes a way of life for them. They always seem to be at the right place at the right time and are very aware that the seemingly innocuous coincidences actually are clues to what their next action should be, and whom and what they should align themselves with.

For example, you experience a coincidence if you are at work and you keep running into the same person in the elevator, or if you have someone that you would really like to meet and they suddenly show up in front of you. These are examples of seemingly random interactions that could actually have meaning to them. Perhaps that person whom you keep running into on the elevator is supposed to mentor you to help you to get your next promotion or make a very important introduction to someone that would be impactful in your life. The person that you had a fleeting thought of wanting to meet who shows up without a planned meeting certainly has a real role to play in your life.

This sort of thing happens in my life as often as it does in most people's lives. The difference is that I have learned to really pay attention and act on it. I'll share two short stories with you to illustrate two such incidents. To protect the identity of some, I've change their names for purposes of recounting this. In 2009 I had gone to a meeting with a dear friend and colleague who was the COO of a large company. This was a business meeting to bounce off some ideas on how I could obtain additional capital in order to scale my company and have some general discussion around increasing efficiencies and strategically targeting additional clients to expand our base.

The COO, Daniel, said to me, "Have you ever met Edie Fraser?" I said no, but that I had heard of her name in the past and that it rang a strong bell. He proceeded to tell me that I absolutely had to meet her and that she would be a great person to be connected to. He said she was extremely well connected and really cared about and took a strong interest in the success and advancement of women. I wrote down her name, as I always do when I either hear a name or something that strikes me to be important, and I felt in my heart that I would meet her at some point.

After that meeting I went back to the office and started to map out strategy around our discussion and came up with a road map of how to implement some of Daniel's suggestions. In going through my notes I saw Edie's name and felt a photographic click sound go off in my mind, and then I went about other business.

A year passed, and I was attending a large conference in Washington, DC, that I was not scheduled to attend, but was invited to as a guest of one of my clients at the last minute. It was a great conference where I met some very inspiring people as well as some future clients.

During the luncheon, I heard the person at the podium say, "We have a special treat today, and our guest keynote speaker is Edie Fraser." My ears immediately perked up, and I was a little surprised. Since it was a last-minute decision to attend I hadn't done my normal due diligence on the list of speakers and attendees. At that moment, I felt an inner voice nudge me and say "Remember, that's the woman Daniel mentioned to you last year at the coffee shop." She was a captivating speaker and I felt a connection to her.

But there were over one thousand attendees at the conference, so the likelihood of me being able to talk with her that day was very slim. She spoke and then left the room. I thought to myself, "Hopefully I will get to connect with her one day, as I feel this is not a coincidence that I ended up at this conference that I had no plans to attend and she is the keynote speaker."

We finished lunch and had to go downstairs to get to the breakout sessions. Fortunately I stopped near a conference room to make a phone call, because as I was about to step back on the escalator I looked to my left and Edie Fraser was standing right next to me! What are the odds of this? I then knew without a shadow of a doubt that we were meant to connect and I looked over and said, "Edie, you and I are meant to talk, and this meeting is long overdue." She smiled and said, "Sounds good, here is my card—call me next week to set up a meeting."

The rest is history. Edie has been one of my strongest mentors and has been a catalyst in the success that I have experienced through her introductions to people, as well as aligning me with the right opportunities at the right time. She is a trusted advisor and a very dear friend. Had I not been present during my meeting with Daniel, been mindful of what was happening around me and trusted my intuition, we would have probably never crossed paths.

Another great story is how I met my agent, Bill Gladstone. In 2011, I was at one of Deepak Chopra's profound meditation retreats in Sedona, and one of the guest teachers was the very famous and prolific author, Jean Houston. I was fortunate enough to meet her, but I think you are getting the point that this happens to me a lot. Our meeting was completely by chance, We happened to be walking down the same hall one day and our paths thankfully crossed.

She asked me how I was enjoying the session and asked me to tell her a bit about myself. I told her that I was really inspired and was exposed and introduced to dormant parts of myself, and I was very grateful for that. I also told her that I was writing a book and she smiled a very knowing smile and nodded her head. I told her what it was about, and she gave me her personal home phone number and offered to provide any assistance I needed in terms of another set of eyes on my manuscript or if I had any questions about the process. I was extremely grateful.

Just as we were about to part she said, "Once you have your book proposal completed let me know, and I will get it to my agent Bill Gladstone." I was so happy. Her generosity warmed my heart. I had heard of Bill Gladstone and knew he was Eckhart Tolle's agent, and now that I found out he was Jean's agent as well, I was floored. I thought that I would probably not get access to him if it weren't for her.

Those who have had the distinct pleasure of becoming acquainted with Jean Houston know she is nothing short of amazing. One of her many gifted abilities is to be able to sense not only your strengths, but your challenges and provide such incredible insight as to how to navigate through your personal journey despite them. I have learned to always take these opportunities to speak to people that I feel drawn to and not hold back. Hopefully by the time you are at this page of my book, a flood of encounters in your life have come crashing to the forefront of your mind, and you are putting together the pieces of the intricately woven puzzle of your life.

2012 came around when I was at Miraval Resort in Arizona, a truly magical place I mentioned earlier. I went to an astrological consultation with one of the most energetically positive and accurate astrologers that I have ever had the pleasure to share space with, Carolyn Crawford. After our enlightening session, I mentioned to her that I was writing a book and told her what it was about and that I was working on the formal book proposal.

She asked me if I had ever read the book *The Golden Motorcycle Gang*. When I said that I had not, she said that the authors were Jack Canfield and Bill Gladstone, and that in addition to being a successful movie producer and author Bill was an amazing agent to very prolific authors. I felt that nudge from my intuition again. I said, "Yes! I am familiar with him, but have never met him." She didn't say anything further about it, and we went our separate ways.

In 2013 I went to Miraval again and had another enlightening session with Carolyn. It was a year later, and we had not kept in touch, but she remembered me. After the session she asked me how things were going, and I mentioned that things were going well with my book writing, and since the formal book proposal was complete, I was at a point where I needed to find a good agent. She said, "Oh yes! We discussed that last time we met. So glad things are going well."

I mentioned names of a few agents I was considering, including Bill Gladstone. But I told her that Bill, like many great agents, was not accepting new clients. Carolyn said, "Bill Gladstone is a friend of a friend, and I can definitely get your proposal in front of him. Send it to me."

This time I didn't feel a nudge, I felt a shaking of my being and knew without a shadow of a doubt that there was a reason why Carolyn had not brought up her sending my proposal to Bill last year when we met. She was not meant to. The timing wasn't right. Needless to say, I received a call from Bill Gladstone two weeks later, and he said that although he was not currently taking on new clients he was very impressed with my manuscript and saw amazing potential for it.

I knew immediately that this meeting was years in the making, and I told him the story of how we were supposed to meet based on the events that had unfolded over the past few years. He said, "Great . . . let's get started." The rest is history here as well. It has been such a joy working with Bill. His guidance and experience is a great asset to me, and I admire how he has his hand on the pulse of not only what is happening now, but what will be successful and impactful.

I hope that you can tangibly see how being present makes a positive, tangible impact on all aspects of your life—from your ability to excel at work to being present in your family and social life. Being present is an essential ingredient to living an extraordinary life.

- Take clear mental and physical notes of the seemingly unimportant coincidences that unfold in your life.
- The most important person in your life is the person that is in front of you at any given moment.
- Be mindful of your surroundings
- Listen to your inner voice.

## Cultivating the Art of Being Present

### *Breathing Exercise: Alternate Nostril Breathing*

I have yet to find a better exercise to bring me in the present moment than *Anuloma Viloma* (Alternate Nostril Breathing). Everyone discusses the importance of being present, but how does one do that? I do that by inhaling and exhaling and bringing my attention to that action. When you do that you are immediately brought to the present moment. As a daily part of my meditation practice, I start by doing this. It really calms and balances the mind. Try to do ten rounds of this daily.

Please note that the exhalation is twice as long as the inhalation, and this enables all the toxins and stale air to exit from the lungs and your entire body as an added benefit. Following are the steps to perform this exercise. It does not take long and will have an immediate effect on your sense of well-being.

### How to Perform *Anuloma Viloma*

- First, take your right hand bend the two middle fingers into your palm. The thumb will be used to close the right nostril, and the two fingers on the end will be used to close the left one.
- Close the right nostril with your thumb. Exhale through the left nostril and then inhale to a count of four.
- Close the left nostril as well and hold the breath for a count of sixteen.
- Release the right nostril and exhale fully through it to a count of eight.
- Keep the left nostril closed and inhale through the right to a count of four.

- Close the right nostril as well and hold the breath to a count of sixteen.
- Release the left nostril and exhale to a count of eight. This is one round.

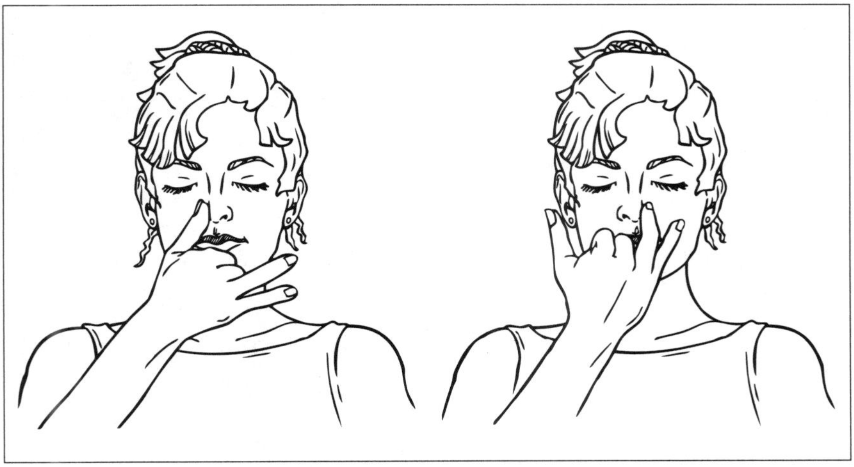

***Anuloma Viloma***
(Alternate Nostril Breathing)

# THE STREAM OF LIFE

*The same stream of life*
*that runs through my veins*
*runs through the world*
*and dances in rhythmic measure.*
*It is the same life*
*that shoots in joy*
*through the dust of the earth*
*into numberless blades of grass,*
*and breaks into tumultuous waves*
*of leaves and flowers.*
*It is the same life that is rocked*
*in the ocean cradle*
*of birth and death,*
*in ebb and in flow.*
*My limbs are made glorious*
*by the touch of this world of life;*
*and my pride is from*
*the life throb of ages*
*dancing in my blood this moment.*

—Tagore

Trait 2

# BE OPEN TO SERENDIPITY

*When I am, as it were, completely myself, entirely alone, and of good cheer—say traveling in a carriage, or walking after a good meal, or during the night when I cannot sleep—it is on such occasions that my ideas flow best, and most abundantly. Whence and how they come, I know not, nor can I force them.*—MOZART

In business, we generally feel that there is a certain path to take to achieve or goal or complete the project. There are steps and processes that have been put in place, which have proven to be successful time and time again, and we decide to follow those—almost blindly. In order to continue to be marketable, the companies who came up with the processes merely upgrade their versions to version 5.0 and convince us that they have been able to do a catch-all to account for any sort of evolution. How can this be possible when there are infinite possibilities?

It's not that there isn't anything to learn from those processes; it's rather that those processes were derived at a certain point in time, and are based on a certain particular set of circumstances and people that came up with them. The more productive way to apply these would be to learn from history by reviewing them and seeing what things both are applicable now and resonate with you. Believe it or not, half of what makes a project or initiative successful is that fact that the people involved are what we call "all-in." They are fully vested in the success of the project: mind, body, and spirit. They are not just going through the motions. They believe in the initiative and they feel that they have contributed to the path to achieve it with their own personal touch. You will rarely see a successful project where the members of the team are just marking time or collecting a paycheck.

***Believe it or not, half of what makes a project or initiative successful is that fact that the people involved are what we call "all-in." They are fully vested in the success of the project: mind, body, and spirit. They are not just going through the motions.***

Think about all of the projects or things you have achieved that you consider successful. Did you follow a pre-determined road map to get there? Probably not. Most of the time it is the path that hasn't even shown itself that is the best one for us to take. Many of us have taken the unconventional path that revealed itself to us, and that is what made all the difference. However, this path is usually not the one that appears with a bright flashing light above it that says, "The road to success—enter here." This path is one that if you had really tried to plan things out, you probably would not have chosen. This is where Serendipity usually comes in and shows her face. If you are open to and cognizant of serendipity, you can let in unlimited possibilities.

***All serendipitous events only happen after we have opened our minds to the possibility that things can be done another way and that perhaps the way that we had thought initially or even what we thought about the entire subject may not be the right way.***

Serendipity is something that is not so easily defined. According to Wikipedia it is defined by "a fortuitous happenstance" or a "pleasant surprise." I feel it goes to levels that are much deeper and unchartered than this. This definition implies that there is no rhyme or reason for it, that it is random, and it is positive. But I think serendipity has a major component to it that is not found in any common definition—Energy. The energy associated with serendipity is one that comes from within and is not external. It comes from within because all serendipitous events only happen after we have opened our minds to the possibility that things can be done another way and that perhaps the way that we had thought initially or even what we thought about the entire subject may not be the right way. If we do not open our minds to those possibilities, serendipity can never occur.

## Fixed Mindset versus Growth Mindset

A series of interesting studies by Dr. Carol Dwek, Professor of Psychology at Stanford University, shed some light on a potential reason as to why we might not be as open as often as we should be. She studied athletes and students. She found that there are two distinct mentalities of people. She coined the terms "Fixed Mindset" and "Growth Mindset." Those individuals with a fixed mindset believed that abilities of people are fixed and that they are like gifts—you either have them or you don't. Those with a growth mindset, in contrast, believe that these abilities can be cultivated through practice. It is clear to them that there are some people that may achieve things faster than others, but in time everyone is capable of being successful in what they set out to do.

She further found that those with a fixed mindset were convinced that their abilities were not only finite, but that they as people were defined by the certain amount that they had. They felt the need to try to make themselves look amazing at all times and hide or mask any shortcomings or deficiencies. They would even avoid taking on any opportunity to learn something new or become more proficient at something as they feared being exposed. But those with the growth mindset welcomed the ability and opportunity to learn something new and felt that it enhanced their abilities and helped them potentially master a particular skill.

Those with a fixed mindset didn't really care about learning per se; they cared about being right or wrong and felt that that fact defined their success. When they were right in solving a particular problem on a test, they were happy, and when they were wrong they felt defeated. When they were right, they didn't even care where they were right to use it as a further learning opportunity—they were just happy they were right. This affected them significantly in a negative way in their next performance.

As we all know, life is full of moments of a perceived success "being right" and a perceived defeat "being wrong." How one copes with this is what matters. Those in the fixed mindset after doing poorly on a test actually said they would put forth less effort and possibly study less since they felt it really wouldn't make any difference.

Those with the growth mindset also cared about being right or wrong. However, when they were right they cared equally about *which* things they were right about, and when they were wrong they wanted to understand *why* and learn from it. This mentality helped them in subsequent tests as they could apply the process and what they had learned to the next one. They fared much better on the next test than the fixed mindset group. Their view on a setback or a perceived defeat motivated them to put forth more effort and to regroup and perhaps study differently. They were determined to do well and overcome the challenge.

She further examined where these mindsets and mentalities came from. Interestingly, it came from the type of feedback the students got. When the students were given feedback that was more "person" driven, such as "Great job! You are so smart," they were more inclined to stick to doing the thing that got them this response so that they could hear it again and not risk losing future accolades. They adopted more of a fixed mindset.

However, when the students got feedback that lauded the "process" rather than the "person," they wanted to take on more challenges and actually go after the things that would enable them to learn more. They adopted a more growth-oriented mindset when they were complimented on how they went about doing something and how creative they were.

You can take the information from these studies and examine how you personally tackle a project or a challenge that you are faced with. Do you only volunteer for projects at the office that you think you can excel in to look good, or do you join the teams that might have a challenge that has not been solved for an extended period of time and try to see what value you can add? By doing this you also realize that you learn more and expand your mind while adding value. You can allow your creative juices to flow as they are ripened by the challenge.

Those that focus on adding value rather than receiving accolades are those who get promoted and noticed by upper management. Surprisingly, it matters infinitely less to those that are watching if you hit a few bumps in the road. It matters much more how many times you got in the car, the difference you make, and your overall track record. Wouldn't you want someone on your team who really cared about the success of the group and that put in genuine effort to achieve the collective goal, rather than someone who was deemed a superstar but really only cared about looking good? The life span of the "superstar" that only cares about his or her personal success, is one that is very short-lived and also mostly not impactful. They are the one-hit-wonders of the world. They don't go multi-platinum. Ever.

***It matters infinitely less to those that are watching if you hit a few bumps in the road. It matters much more how many times you got in the car, the difference you make, and your overall track record.***

These studies were also very interesting to me as they clearly illustrate the constrictiveness of being "fixed" and the expansiveness of being "growth" oriented. You can feel the box being created around you when you close your mind to possibilities. In contrast to this, when you are open you feel free and that the world is your oyster. You breathe more expansively and deeply. The horizon seems very far away and you marvel at the space before you. You feel you can accomplish anything you set out to because you will put in the effort that is required, as well as open your mind to the creative process.

If you are open and not attached to an outcome you can let in unlimited possibilities. This also opens the space for random seemingly coincidental events to occur that then proceed to shape our lives. A million dollar deal could become a billion dollar deal. However, if we are closed to that possibility, then there is so much creativity that is being repressed and opportunity that could be lost. That billion dollar deal? It can vanish in a second.

## Cultivating the Art of Being Open to Serendipity

Letting go of a fixed idea of what your path to success should take or look like can actually lead to greater opportunities beyond your wildest imagination. Open yourself to Serendipity, and it will bring you gifts that you never even dreamed of. You can cultivate the inner energy of Serendipity by consciously practicing being open and letting go at the same time. When faced with a challenge, clear your mind and listen to the ideas around you as well as your own inner voice.

Let go of any preconceived notions. It is actually something that is easier done than said when you allow yourself to be present and open to the possibilities. When you realize that Serendipity is cultivated and that you can practice this daily, you will become addicted to the sweet elixir that you have tasted and will keep coming back for more.

Remember, the face of success changes for us and how it appears to us as we evolve. It does not remain fixed. What we may view as successful for us at one moment could not be several months or years from now. Priorities change, our emotional intelligence evolves, and the landscape of our innermost desires adjusts in real time as well. When we realize this, the chase actually stops and we enjoy the moment that we are in and we are open to the possibilities of what it will bring through the energy of Serendipity.

***Remember, the face of success changes for us and how it appears to us as we evolve. It does not remain fixed.***

## Yoga Poses: Seated Chest Lift and Seated Forward Bend

The yoga pose of Seated Chest Lift, or a modified version of *Dandasana*, that I have chosen is one that opens your chest and heart center. This is the place where one must be open in order to be open to serendipity. This is a great pose to do at the office in a chair as many of us are hunched over a computer for an extended period of time. I will also suggest a counter pose to some of the yoga poses that will balance your spine.

The counter pose to Seated Chest Lift is Seated Forward Bend, or *Uttanasana* in Sanskrit. *Uttanasana* is usually done standing, but I will show a seated version on the next pages since I feel that it would be easier since you will already be seated.

***Seated Chest Lift***
(Modified Dandasana)

## Seated Chest Lift *(Modified Dandasana)*

- Choose a comfortable seated position (legs extended straight in front, or even sitting on a chair with your feet flat on the floor). Keep your spine straight, and position your hands behind your back alongside your hips, and press your fingertips into the ground. If you are in a chair, place your hands on either side of the chair alongside your hips, and press your fingertips into the chair.
- Inhale slowly, raise your chest straight up, and close your eyes and gently tilt your head back.
- You should feel your spine lengthening and an openness in your chest and heart center—opening you to serendipity.
- Exhale and bring your head back to the neutral position. Repeat this a few more times.

***Seated Forward Bend***

## Seated Forward Bend (counter pose of Seated *Uttanasana*)

- In your comfortable seated position after you have completed your Chest Lifts and have returned to neutral, bend forward, reaching your arms in front of you and spreading your fingertips on the ground or grabbing your legs or feet. If you are in a chair, just fold forward and either hang like a rag doll or touch the floor.
- Relax here for a few breaths, and feel the opening in your hips and your mind and spirit ready to face the day and be open to serendipity.

***Eagle Pose***
(Garudasana)

## Yoga Pose: Eagle Pose *(Garudasana)*

Eagle pose is normally a standing pose. However, I really like to do this pose in a seated position at my desk. It opens up your shoulders and creates a much-needed space between the shoulder blades. For those of us who sit in front of a desk for hours on end while typing, reading, or writing, this pose works wonders to counteract the debilitating effects of the repetitive poor posture and strain injuries that result from doing these activities for extended periods of time.

While sitting comfortably in your chair, sit up straight and plant your feet firmly on the ground creating a 90-degree angle. Then, place your arms in front of you and bend your elbows at a 90-degree angle. Cross your arms so that the right arm is above the left. Interlock your arms and press your palms together with your fingertips pointing toward the ceiling.

You will feel an incredible stretch. Then repeat the movement by alternatively crossing your left arm above the right as well to get the best effect. This pose strengthens your triceps, shoulders, and back muscles. This pose is also used by many as a preventative measure of the problem of carpal tunnel syndrome. If you are able, you can cross your legs and interlock them with one foot behind the other. This part is not required.

# YOUR TEACUP IS FULL
## (empty your cup)

*Once, a long time ago, there was a wise Zen master. People from far and near would seek his counsel and ask for his wisdom. Many would come and ask him to teach them, enlighten them in the way of Zen. He seldom turned any away.*

*One day an important man and highly educated man, came to visit the master. "I have come today to ask you to teach me about Zen. Open my mind to enlightenment." The tone of the important man's voice was one used to getting his own way.*

*The Zen master smiled and said that they should discuss the matter over a cup of tea. When the tea was served the master poured his visitor a cup. He poured and he poured and the tea rose to the rim and began to spill over the table and finally onto the robes of the wealthy man. Finally the visitor shouted, "Enough. You are spilling the tea all over. Can't you see the cup is full?"*

*The master stopped pouring and smiled at his guest. "Like this cup you are full of your own opinions and speculations. How can I show you Zen unless you first empty your cup?" How can I show you Zen unless you first empty your cup?"*

—Buddhist Parable

## Trait 3

# CHANGE YOUR PERCEPTION, CHANGE YOUR REALITY

*Do not let anyone rent space in your head for free.*

—powerful words from my late father

Often we have so much anxiety over an encounter that we had with someone or what an upcoming meeting will be like. If we really tell ourselves and believe that we are merely perceiving this situation to be anxiety provoking, and it is not the reality, we will begin to feel so much more calm and at ease. One distinction that separates those people that have The OM Factor and those who do not is the ability to *respond* rather than *react* to a situation.

Those with the OM Factor can do this because they are not standing there fuming and holding their breath with anger or anxiety. They are in the present moment and they are experiencing exactly what is happening without passing judgment on it. They are having a conversation and listening to what the other party is saying and then, because they are able to breathe normally, they can think clearly and respond.

It is not that these people do not feel or experience emotion; it is that they don't react to their emotions. They witness the emotion and then respond to what is said rather than how it is said. When you do this you can respond with something that adds value, keeps your blood pressure in check, and also changes the entire dynamic of the conversation.

Understand that your perception is your reality. Your perception of a situation will determine your physical, emotional, and mental state. So make sure you are mindful to tell yourself when things get volatile that it is merely your perception, and as your perception changes, so will the reality. This is **key** for dealing with anxiety. As we learned in part two when discussing the third tool, anxiety causes a great deal of stress to our body, mind, and spirit.

***It is not that these people do not feel or experience emotion; it is that they don't* react *to their emotions. They* witness *the emotion and then respond to what is said rather than how it is said.***

Part two gave us the tools to deal with it in the moment by using affirmations and mantras. This chapter on the trait of the ability to change our perceptions will help us cultivate our OM Factor in this area so that we have to use those tools less and less as we will learn to perceive a stressful situation differently from the onset, and not experience that level of anxiety and stress on ourselves and in our bodies.

Let's be honest: there are some events that are anxiety provoking and mentally debilitating to most human beings, such as the death of someone dear to us. This is universally considered to be a major life event that is thankfully not part of the daily experiences and interactions that happen in our lives. The majority of what we experience and how we experience it largely depends on our perception of the situation.

For example, at Technalink we have a lot of projects that need to be staffed up very quickly with very qualified resources. We do not carry a large bench and need to be able to acquire talent from the outside to work on these engagements. We have a small, yet extraordinarily nimble and effective talent acquisition team. Many times we are awarded a project that needs to have a team ready to go and engaged within seven–ten days. This is not an easy task by any stretch, but it lends itself to be a great example of a daily stressor to say the least. Our internal process, post-award goes like this: We celebrate. Then, we have a post-award, kick-off meeting with our internal team and map out exactly what the skill sets are of the resources that we need to engage on the project. Then, we divide up the tasks and get to work.

Here is where the perception of the daily stressor of finding these people quickly comes into play. Once I walked into the offices of the team and saw two people on the same team, with the same task, perceive and therefore react to this as complete polar opposites. One person smiled and said, "Great! Let's get to work!" She proceeded to organize her time and map out a plan as to whom in her network she was going to reach out to for referrals as well as contact others that were available in the marketplace.

The second individual said, "I don't see how we are going to be able to find ten people in two weeks. I hope the client understands the project may get pushed out to the right a bit." I thought, "How interesting." How could two people that were doing the exact same task with the exact same amount of work react so completely differently?

I went to my office and started to recount other situations perceived as stressful that occurred in our workplace, and I thought back to how each of these two individuals reacted to them. In most instances, one of them not only had a wonderful can-do attitude, but her actions would take on a tone of achievement. It was as if she already had accomplished the task at hand and she perceived everything was a creative opportunity to make a difference. The second person, in most instances that I could recount, had a very pessimistic and almost resigned attitude to anything that was presented to her. It was as if she was unable to see beyond the "work" aspect of the task, and perceived things to be a chore rather than an opportunity to not only personally grow, but also help the company evolve.

I met with the second individual to ask her about how things were going for her and if she was happy. That is a very subjective and yet deep question to ask someone. The answer to this question also depends on your perception of what is going on in your life as well as your perception of yourself. For some, this changes from moment to moment as they are self-described as a "work in progress" and continuously try to cultivate a positive, evolutionary response to everything rather than just reacting.

For others, their perception of the state of their lives is immutable. They accept their reality as it is as if everything is happening to them, and they are the victims of the experiences. They feel they have no real role to play, other than feeling sorry that their lives have turned out this way and they need to learn to live with it.

She immediately reacted and said, "Why are you asking? Is something wrong? Did I do something wrong?" That reaction was very telling. She immediately went toward the pessimistic side of things and thought she was going to be fired. I explained to her that there was no agenda to my questions, and that I genuinely wanted to know if she was happy with her job and life in general. She then settled into her chair a bit and said, "I don't think I am. I am not happy with a lot of things in my life right now." I listened to her exhale her thoughts to me. I think she honestly was truly breathing for the first time.

She thanked me for listening. We came to the conclusion that she should pursue a different aspect of talent acquisition. Unfortunately, we did not have an opening or need for this at the time, and I told her I would put her in touch with a few people in my network that might. I suggested to her that she may want to address other aspects of her life in the same way we did her career path, and that she would probably feel a lot more happiness after she aligned herself with people and choices that served her as opposed to those that were toxic. She agreed and said she would do that right away.

I had never seen her so motivated to do something! She had a spring in her step, and she genuinely smiled, not only externally. I could feel her heart smiling. She is no longer with Technalink, but I hear she is thriving at another firm, is in a healthier relationship, and is mentoring other women in the workplace. It is not that there are no challenges in her new job, but she is clearly perceiving them differently.

## Cultivating the Art of Altering Our Perceptions to Change Our Reality

It is amazing how doing a little introspection and being honest with yourself about the details of what transpired in a situation can shed so much light on why you may have just reacted to a situation instead of responded to it mindfully. When you take away your ego and sit in silence, you allow your highest self to emerge and illuminate the situation for you. The perceived darkness was only there because your eyes were closed, and the clouds of judgment were hiding the light of the beautiful sun that was trying to peek through. The person that stands to gain from changing your perception and thereby changing your reality, is first and foremost YOU.

So many times we perceive that if we change, the other person has won. Some common thoughts are "Why should I change? Why can't they? They are the ones who caused the problem in the first place. If the person hadn't said or done that I wouldn't have reacted that way, and we wouldn't be in this mess." Sound familiar? First of all, if you wait for that to happen chances are you will be waiting for a very long time. Secondly, why should someone else determine how long you are going to feel miserable inside? Why not take charge of your life and realize that your perception of the situation may be key to your own

***So many times we perceive that if we change, the other person has won.***

personal happiness and also the single most important thing that will change your reality.

In an instant, you can go from being miserable to being happy. Think back to a time when you went from a miserable state to a happy one. I am sure, when you look back, that shift did not happen because the situation changed. That shift happened because you consciously decided that you were tired of feeling that way and that you wanted to feel happy again. You then took steps to change that internal perception as my former employee did, and you consciously changed your reality.

I am not suggesting that the other person may not be wrong or that he or she is behaving in a manner that is appropriate. I am simply suggesting that you take them out of the equation for a minute and observe the situation and your role in shaping the outcome and subsequently your reality. When you do this, **you win** because you reclaim your life. You no longer exist in a series of reactive moments, but rather you live a life full of meaningful, mindful, and empowering ones.

Dr. Richard S. Lazarus, the influential professor and researcher in the Department of Psychology at the University of California, Berkeley until 1991, was a pioneer in the study of emotion and stress. In his work on coping strategies, he put it very persuasively: "Stress resides neither in the situation nor in the person, it depends on a transaction between the two."

He found that the daily anxieties such as work tensions, sitting in traffic, and performing mundane household chores could affect a person's blood pressure and cause other physical symptoms such as chest pain, or bringing on asthma attacks. He also linked the risk of the perception of these daily anxieties to getting infections. He said,

"If you are an inept coper or a person who overacts, then your stress level will be higher and so will your risk of infectious illness."

Dr. Richard S. Lazarus conducted several studies on the beliefs of a person and how the individual perceived a situation to be, and he determined that these beliefs can either have a very positive or negative consequence for one's health and well-being. Based on these studies, he urged that medical professionals must take the emotional and physiological reactions into account and bring them into the fold of the discussion and subsequent plan for achieving good health.

You have the opportunity to decide how to respond and perceive every situation. When you react by losing control of your emotions, you then give up your power to the other person. Your greatest strength is the ability to choose your response and control your perception of things. By consciously changing your perception, you indeed change your reality.

***You have the opportunity to decide how to respond and perceive every situation. When you react by losing control of your emotions, you then give up your power to the other person.***

***Warrier 2***
(Virbhadrasana 2)

## Yoga Pose: Warrior 2 (*Virabhadrasana 2*)

This trait is one of empowerment, and I cannot think of a better empowerment posture than Warrior 2 (*Virabhadrasana* 2 in Sanskrit). Virabhadra is the name of a fierce warrior, an incarnation of Shiva, described as having 1,000 heads, a 1,000 eyes and 1,000 feet, wielding 1,000 clubs, and wearing a tiger's skin. Now that image is definitely powerful. This pose strengthens your legs and arms, opens your chest and shoulders, and tones your abdomen. This pose also improves your focus, balance, and sense of stability—energizing your entire body.

- Start by standing with your feet slightly apart and take a few deep breaths with your eyes closed. When you feel comfortable gently open your eyes.
- Step your feet fairly wide: about three to four feet apart, and raise your arms parallel to the floor and reach them out to the sides with your palms facing down.
- Turn your right foot slightly to the right and your left foot slightly inward so that your hips and shoulders are facing your left foot.
- Bend your right knee so that your thigh is parallel to the ground and your knee is not hyperextended over your toes.
- Stay here for a minute or about ten-twelve nice long breaths.
- Inhale and lift your arms straight up so that you are facing front with your legs still apart in Warrior 2 position.
- Exhale and lower back down to Warrior 2. Repeat this sequence, and then reverse your feet and do the routine again on the other side.
- Feel your inner strength and confidence throughout your entire body. You are ready to choose consciously and wisely and create your own reality.

# DAILY AWARENESS POEM

*Always we hope*
*someone else has the answer.*
*Some other place will be better,*
*some other time it will all turn out.*
*This is it.*
*No one else has the answer.*
*No other place will be better,*
*and it has already turned out.*
*At the center of your being*
*you have the answer;*
*you know who you are*
*and you know what you want.*
*There is no need*
*to run outside*
*for better seeing.*
*Nor to peer from a window.*
*Rather abide at the center of your being;*
*for the more you leave it, the less you learn.*
*Search your heart*
*and see*
*the way to do*
*is to be.*

—Lao Tzu

## Trait 4

# DIGEST YOUR THOUGHTS CREATIVELY

Your state of mind dictates the state of your body. We digest our thoughts in the belly of our consciousness as we do our food. When we have thoughts that come from a place of love they digest easily, and we pass that which no longer serves us. When we have toxic thoughts, or thoughts that do not come from love, they can cause ulcer-like manifestations in our consciousness.

Internal strife and toxic thoughts wreak havoc on the physical body. For instance, when you are happy your skin looks great, your body is in shape, your breathing is very rhythmic, your eyes even smile. All of your internal systems are functioning in harmony. When your state of mind is not clear, your skin breaks out, your shoulders cave in from bad posture, and your breathing is shallow or hyperactive. It is clear even by looking in the mirror that things are not functioning properly.

Other more serious problems result when we allow these negative thoughts to fester. Our stomach churns, our chest burns, and we chomp on antacids to pacify the problem. But if we fail to deal with the root of the problem, we will manifest for ourselves a great big ulcer. Remember, life is not just happening to us as passive bystanders. We are actively digesting it. Every directed comment from someone else, every internal self-dialogue, every experience that we have in this physical world is actively digested. The thing is, we cannot change what is said or experienced, but we can change how we process that. That is something that is completely in our control.

While growing up, most of us have heard our parents or someone elder to us say, "Chew your food . . . slowly . . . don't just gulp it down and swallow it." There is serious merit to that advice. Both physically and mentally. Chewing our food slowly allows us to taste the food and determine if it is sweet, salty, sour, bitter, astringent, or pungent. It allows our bodies to actually produce more saliva that mixes in with the food to allow for better processing and digestion. It allows our minds to determine whether the food we are eating is something that we like or something that we would rather never try again.

***Remember, life is not just happening to us as passive bystanders. We are actively digesting it. Every directed comment from someone else, every internal self-dialogue, every experience that we have in this physical world is actively digested.***

Swallowing our food whole, when we are in a hurry at work or at home, doesn't allow for any of this. You cannot taste a thing when you swallow it. The texture of the food may be felt, but you could honestly swallow a piece of tofu and then a piece of chicken, and they would almost taste the same. Our stomachs then have a lot more work to do. They have to break down something much bigger in size than it would have been if we swallowed it, and we end up feeling very uncomfortable and bloated.

A very good example of this digestion process can be shown in the workplace. Let's say there is a conference call at the office where executive leadership will be present, and the call is to not only brief them on how the various projects are performing, but also to strategize on how to create efficiencies and increase company profit. You are a manager and your senior manager is also on the phone.

You begin to go through each project and discuss the things that are going well and the things that could stand to be improved and you provide context of how you are dealing with those challenges. You are extremely prepared for the call and feel that everyone is receiving your message well.

All of a sudden your senior manager, whom you directly report to, starts to ask some more deep-dive questions. You had a meeting prior to the call to go over the details of the status of the projects, and she was very aware of the state of affairs. She surprisingly asks things that she clearly knows the answer to because you and she had discussed them in your previous meeting. You immediately start to feel confused and angry as to why she would be doing this on a call with executive management. It felt inside as though she was questioning your abilities. You answer her questions since there are several people on the conference call, and after a couple of iterations the conversation concludes.

Afterward you sit in your office still thinking about the call and not feeling great like you did before she asked the questions. Instead, you feel slighted and potentially sabotaged. You start to fester and internally begin to boil inside. She passes by your office and ducks her head in and says, "Great call just now. I think it went well." Then she continues down the hallway—as if nothing happened. "I think it went well? Did she just say that?" you think to yourself.

You begin to think about it further and are convinced that she was definitely trying to make you look incompetent in front of executive leadership and resentment comes and takes its place at the table next to anger. By this time she has made her way back down the hall smiling and with a seeming skip in her step. It infuriates you.

You say, "Jen, can I speak to you for a minute." She says "sure" and sits down. You begin to share your feelings about the call with her and how you feel that she has directly violated your trust. Further, you tell her that she was actively trying to make you look bad in front of executive leadership. Her eyes widen as you are delivering this diatribe and she is silent until you finish. She says, calmly, "Wow . . . that was not at all my intention. I was trying to bring up those things since you hadn't mentioned them in the call. I was so impressed with the way that you handled them and I wanted to make sure each and every one of them were discussed in detail.

"I wanted leadership to see that you have a lot of dimension and are completely on top of everything and can see the forest through the trees as well as be in the weeds if needed. I had a meeting with them last week where I recommended a promotion to senior management for you, as you excel on every level in my eyes and get along with our clients. I have a great deal of respect for you and your abilities."

Your jaw drops, and simultaneously so does your head, and you just stare at the floor. You are feeling like a complete fool and wish you could rewind the last fifteen minutes and hit the restart button. The problem is you can't. You profusely apologize and explain where you were coming from. She thankfully, graciously accepts your apology and explanation and says she understands.

Had you taken a few minutes and not immediately assumed the worst and essentially swallowed your food whole, but had instead experienced the food by chewing it—the outcome would have been totally different. You too, would have smiled when you both met after the call, and both of you would have said, "That went well, didn't it?"

All of the negative physical and mental things that occurred in your mind and body would not have happened, and they would have been replaced by feelings of fulfillment, appreciation, and happiness. Swallowing our food or interactions whole without chewing them allows them to enter our stomachs or lives, but the entire experience is different, isn't it? The same piece of food or interaction can end up having a positive impact and be a very positive experience or have a decidedly detrimental impact and be a very negative one.

## Epigenetics and Our Subconscious Mind

Cultivating this trait of digesting your thoughts creatively is one that comes from both conscious practice and working "after hours" on your subconscious. Our subconscious minds really control the show. The reciting of the mantras and affirmations truly help us in the moment and are absolutely necessary in getting us back on track. Those are all performed by the conscious mind. However, our subconscious minds actually digest those affirmations and mantras and our beliefs that have been ingrained in us from when we were very young.

Dr. Bruce Lipton, renowned stem cell biologist and internationally recognized leader in bridging the gap between science and spirit, has really been a pioneer for this concept. His research on epigenetics, which is the study of how environmental factors can affect gene expression, is very interesting. His epigenetics research shows that "genes and DNA do not control our biology; instead DNA is controlled by signals from outside the cell, including the energetic messages emanating from our positive and negative thoughts."*His research shows that you can literally change your cell's destiny by altering your thoughts.

For example, if you have been given six months to live and you begin reciting affirmations such as "I am healthy, I am thriving, I am happy," they will absolutely have an effect on your conscious mind and you will feel better at that moment. However, if you believe that the diagnosis is correct and that you will die in six months, chances are you probably will. "That is called the nocebo effect," Lipton says, "the result of a negative thought, which is the opposite of the placebo effect, where healing is mediated by a positive thought." Your subconscious mind controls this part. Lipton further states, "The function of the mind is to create coherence between our beliefs and the reality we experience. What that means is that your mind will adjust the body's biology and behavior to fit with your beliefs."

---

*Source: Bruce H. Lipton, PhD. *The Biology of Belief: Unleashing the Power of Consciousness, Matter, & Miracles.*

I have seen this firsthand. Someone very dear to me was told that his liver was failing and that if he didn't get a transplant within the next month he would have six months to live. He is a very aware man and practices meditation and mindfulness daily and has for the past forty years. He refused to believe it. He took things into his own hands. He continued his meditation practice daily and went to India to heal holistically and stayed in an Ayurvedic center for about six to eight weeks and actively participated in that way of life.

He came back, and his oncologist could hardly believe his eyes. His liver was functioning fine, and although his prognosis was a death sentence a few months earlier, he was now given a very optimistic prognosis.

## Cultivating the Art of Digesting Our Thoughts Creatively

My dear friend took the diagnosis of a failing liver for exactly what it was, a diagnosis. He made his prognosis one of health, happiness, and vitality. He digested his thoughts creatively. He is still alive twelve years later and is thriving. He never believed the prognosis for his recovery in his subconscious mind. He cultivated that belief through meditation and mindfulness.

Imagine that power . . . you can move mountains! I am not saying by any means that mindfulness and meditation will cure ***all*** ailments and disease or that you should ignore your physician's advice. However, through proven research, they definitely have a positive physical, cognitive, and emotional impact, and in many cases have completely turned the outcome around.

By cultivating this trait of digesting your thoughts creatively through practicing meditation daily, you will notice that your initial reactions and thoughts when they are digested will be thoughts that are not assassinating ones, but rather evolutionary ones. You will notice that you not only physically and mentally look and feel better, but that others will say that they love being around you, and that you make them feel better after having been in your presence. You will also see that the solutions to many of your challenges spontaneously manifest, as all of your internal systems are functioning in harmony, and creativity will immediately rise to the surface.

***By cultivating this trait of digesting your thoughts creatively through practicing meditation daily, you will notice that your initial reactions and thoughts when they are digested will be thoughts that are not assassinating ones, but rather evolutionary ones.***

## Yoga Pose: Tree Pose *(Vrsasana)*

The Yoga Pose that I have chosen is one that promotes balance. *Tree Pose is like the branches of the tree swaying with the wind; there are many things happening while you are digesting your thoughts. However, also like a tree, you must be rooted and balanced.* This is essential when you are trying to digest your thoughts creatively. You must be balanced and focused in order to have the space to digest and process.

This pose allows us the space to be rooted in focus and maintain a gentle concentration on a single chosen point, which allows us to balance and develop our concentration further. The other thing I love about tree pose is that it gives immediate feedback. If your mind is wandering around, you will know it immediately . . . you will fall. With practice you will not only be able to hold this pose longer, but you will also see the effects of your focus in your daily interactions.

- Begin standing with feet shoulder-width apart. Shift weight to right foot, and raise left foot to let it rest either against the inside of your right ankle (beginner), just above the inside of your right knee (intermediate), or at the top inside of your right thigh (advanced; shown at right). Any of these methods are perfectly acceptable and all will give the desired results.

- For more stability, squeeze the bottom of your left foot and the inside of your right leg together, lift belly in and up, and draw tailbone down. Fix eyes on a single, non-moving spot, and slowly begin to lift your arms above your head. Hold for five–fifteen breaths; then release and repeat on the other side.

***Tree Pose***
(Vrsasana)

# WE ARE WHAT WE THINK

*We are what we think.*
*All that we are arises with our thoughts.*
*With our thoughts we make the world.*
*Speak or act with an impure mind*
*And Trouble will follow you*
*As the wheel follows the ox that draws the cart.*
*We are what we think.*
*All that we are arises with our thoughts.*
*With our thoughts we make the world.*
*Speak or act with a pure mind*
*and happiness will follow you*
*As your shadow, unshakable.*
*"Look how he abused me and beat me,*
*How he threw me down and robbed me."*
*Live with such thoughts and you live in hate.*
*"Look how he abused me and beat me,*
*How he threw me down and robbed me."*
*Abandon such thoughts, and live in love.*

—BUDDHA

## Trait 5

# BE HUMBLE

Realize that you are merely playing a part in this play called Life. You may have a main role, supporting role, or be an extra. You receive the script when you are born and begin to learn your lines and understand your role and what the expectations are of you playing this part. You learn about your relationship to the rest of your cast-mates, and you begin preparing yourself for a performance that is worth watching on the big screen.

Some of your cast-mates haven't even come on the scene yet and will come in different acts and you will have to interact with them as they show up throughout the play. This requires you to be agile, quick on your feet, and mindful of your choices and relationships, as they will create the landscape of your journey.

You do not control the outcome of the choices you make. There is a chain reaction that goes into effect when you make your choice. The choice is made, and it is very akin to hitting a cue ball with a pool stick on a pool table. Depending on the angle and force with which the cue ball is hit with the stick a number of things can happen. It can push the target ball straight into the pocket, it can hit two other balls and then just stay

***You do not control the outcome of the choices you make. There is a chain reaction that goes into effect when you make your choice.***

on the felt, and it can even push another unintended ball into the pocket and follow in right behind it. We can have the best of intentions and also focused intentions when we make a choice, but just as the cue ball can go in various directions and have different impacts when it comes into contact with the pool stick—so can the outcome of our choices.

We tend to take life and our role in it very seriously, as if we control the outcome. When something awful in our life is happening we usually ask a series of questions that go something like this: "Why is this happening to me? What did I do to deserve this? Why can't this person understand me? Why are they not changing?" Those are all very normal questions.

The problem with those questions is that they seek answers that are out of our control. They are answers that are either dependent on another person and their feelings or thoughts—which have nothing to do with us—or they are the universe's way of keeping balance, and we happen to be the casualties of war sometimes—again, nothing to do with us. To truly understand these statements, you must have the element of humility in your being. Even the strongest, richest, most powerful human being is no match for a tidal wave when standing in front of it. Be humble.

The only things that are in our control are our choices, so we need to really be mindful of what we are choosing. We need to be very clear in our minds that regardless of the outcome our choices, our actions are taken for the highest good for all parties involved.

We also need to understand that everything is a choice. You can choose to be happy or to be miserable. You can choose to give up, or realize that the sun rises every day and it brings new possibilities. No one can force us to react a certain way to something; we choose that. We may feel that we had no other choice than to react a certain way or sacrifice something, but we do. We instantly and innately determine our priorities, and our choices truly follow those priorities.

Our priorities also shift as different events occur in our life. That which was important to us last week may not be important to us today, or perhaps we see it in a different light and other things take priority.

***We also need to understand that* everything *is a choice. You can choose to be happy or to be miserable. You can choose to give up, or realize that the sun rises every day and it brings new possibilities.***

We are also sometimes oblivious to, or choose to not acknowledge that, our achievements would not have been possible without the help of others. But this is incredibly humbling to those who appreciate it. The first thing out of some of the most successful people's mouths is, "I would not be where I am today without the help of" or "I stand on the shoulders of . . . ." The funny thing is that the people that help you along the way also make the choice to help you. We are all so interconnected and essentially one when we really analyze this. It becomes a blissful co-dependence with humanity when we realize that if we all just focused on making conscious choices and not taking credit or lamenting the outcome, we would be very happy.

Humility is very similar to nitroglycerin. This small, seemingly insignificant white pill, when placed under the tongue and out of sight, can truly help save someone's life. It is very powerful. It doesn't mind that it is out of the limelight and hidden. It is comfortable knowing that it has a role to play and helps one by providing precious time for the baton to be handed off to the next person or as an element that will be assisting in ultimately saving someone's life.

Humility is a state of equilibrium in your being where you neither underestimate nor overestimate yourself. You view yourself in a very balanced way and are not swayed by excessive praise or negative opinion. You realize that you are merely playing a role, and after making conscious choices, there is nothing left in your control. You are free from the burdens of others opinions of yourself—whether they are good or bad.

All the actors in the play of life are equally important, and it is those that have this insight and understanding that are the most fulfilled, happy, and successful. These people understand that it takes a series of events to happen in a particular divine order to manifest an outcome. They understand that whether it's getting a promotion, experiencing the death of someone dear to them, winning the lottery, having a child, or losing everything—these things have a reason behind them that is beyond and bigger than themselves.

***Humility is a state of equilibrium in your being where you neither underestimate nor overestimate yourself.***

That understanding requires humility. When you have this understanding you don't get "stuck" in the loop of asking questions; you accept what has happened and move forward knowing that something better is in store for you. It is not something that happens easily or is easy to do. However, it is something that helps you separate yourself from the outcome. When you truly experience humility, you realize that all you have done and can do is play your part and the rest is history.

A prevalent misconception about humility is that you have to be self-deprecating or downplay your achievements or skills in order to be humble or be perceived as being humble. First, that is totally and painfully transparent. Secondly, it serves no one and can be really detrimental to how others perceive you with regard to opportunities that they may offer in the future. This could be for a future project, a new job, or even a new relationship of some sort. Humility is having a very balanced estimation of your own skills and abilities. It is a realistic self-awareness that allows you to be cognizant of your strengths and weaknesses and embrace them both equally. As

C.S. Lewis said, *"True humility is not thinking less of yourself; it is thinking of yourself less."*

Humility is a very important trait to have when in a leadership role of any kind—whether that is of a manager, CEO, or parent. It is embracing the positive and negative traits of an individual and enabling the person to perform at her or his personal best. When those that you lead feel that you are there, yet not in the way, it gives them the space that is required for them to shine and thrive. You will see this in any type of operation. If a manager is hovering over his or her team or micromanaging them, it is only to satisfy the manager's own ego. It does no good for the people on the team. They feel smothered and confined. Creativity gets stifled and so does the spirit of the person. For water to flow down the river into the ocean and become part of the larger whole, it needs the space to do that. It cannot be cut off by a dam and confined, or it will forever remain a lake or a river. The full expression of the person never comes to fruition because it is literally cut off.

## Cultivating the Art of Being Humble

There is a term that is used for this type of leadership, and it is called "Servant Leadership." The concept of servant leadership, introduced by Robert K. Greenleaf in his 1970 essay "The Servant as Leader," demonstrates an important trait of humility—getting out of the way:

> The servant-leader *is* servant first . . . It begins with the natural feeling that one wants to serve, to serve *first*. . . . The difference manifests itself in the care taken by the servant-first to make sure that other people's highest priority needs are being served. The best test, and difficult to administer, is: Do those served grow as persons? Do they, *while being served*, become healthier, wiser, freer, more autonomous, more likely themselves to become servants? And, what is the effect on the least privileged

> in society? Will they benefit or at least not be further deprived? The servant-leader shares power, puts the needs of others first and helps people develop and perform as highly as possible.

Even digesting the term "servant leadership" requires humility and allowing your ego to be checked at the door. Most people have a very negative sense of this when they utter or hear the word "servant" because it has had such negative connotation and an actually horrific association to it. However, in the context of *servant leadership*, a person is actually helping others by being the one who serves others while in a leadership role, rather than being the one who has a servant serving her or him.

When you are able to view serving others as the real success in your life, and it actually becomes the thing that brings you inner happiness, you have then made a true impact on humanity. Mahatma Gandhi, the most prolific and impactful leader of the Indian Freedom Movement struggle, personified servant leadership. He spoke about this when he said:

> Service of the poor has been my heart's desire, and it has always thrown me amongst the poor and enabled me to identify myself with them . . . service can have no meaning unless one takes pleasure in it. When it is done for show or for fear of public opinion, it stunts the man and crushes his spirit. Service which is rendered without joy helps neither the servant nor the served. But all other pleasures and possessions pale into nothingness before service which is rendered in a spirit of joy.

You will find that when you practice this type of leadership in whatever you do, and whomever you interact with, you will feel a sense of inner peace and fulfillment. You will all the while make an impact on someone else's life whether it is in their career or their personal journey. What could be better?

***Child's Pose***
(Balasana)

## Yoga Pose: Child's Pose *(Balasana)*

The yoga pose I have chosen here is one that truly surrenders.

This pose is very restorative and is practiced in the very nurturing fetal position. You are folding your body over and surrendering yourself to the earth and all the while nourishing your inner organs and bringing a sense of calm and peace to your nervous system. When you practice this pose daily it lets you physically feel the bowing down to your inner self. Practicing this will help the correlation between action and thought with regards to "servant leadership." I practice this pose daily, and it allows me to really go within and nurture myself while also practicing to nurture others.

### *The Steps*

- Get down on all fours (hands and knees on the floor).
- Sit back slowly, bringing your tailbone down toward your heels. You should feel a gentle stretch in the knees.
- Using a yoga block or a rolled up blanket under your tailbone will reduce the pressure on your knees. Repeat three times.

# THE SALT DOLL

*Once a salt doll went to measure*
*the depth of the ocean.*
*No sooner was it in the water,*
*that it melted.*
*Now who was left to tell the depth?*

*There is a sign*
*of Perfect Knowledge.*
*The seeker becomes silent*
*when It is attained.*

*Then the "I,"*
*which may be likened to the salt doll,*
*melts in the Ocean of*
*Existence-Knowledge-Bliss Absolute,*
*and becomes one with It.*
*Not the slightest trace of distinction is left.*

—Sri Ramakrishna

## Trait 6

# GIVE FREELY AND BE GRATEFUL

We are giving creatures by nature. However, in the business world or in areas of our lives where we are dealing with others, we lose a little of this as we don't want to be taken for granted or taken advantage of. We go against our true basic nature.

This is a common fear of most human beings, but women in particular have an extra dose of this that we take at bedtime. We feel that if we keep giving and agreeing we will be viewed as a "pushover" or won't be able to advance to the next level as we will be perceived as someone that is not standing her ground or someone that has no boundaries and can be easily taken advantage of. The problem here is that we feel internally that giving means "giving-in" and agreeing with means losing our own identity. When you take a minute and read the previous sentence you realize how true that statement rings to most people. However, our higher-selves know that giving is not "giving-in." Giving is actually the biggest gift to yourself because when you give you end up with more than you ever had before. You not only end up with more quantitatively; you end up with more qualitatively as well.

***Our higher-selves know that giving is not "giving-in." Giving is actually the biggest gift to yourself because when you give you end up with more than you ever had before.***

Quantitatively, we can look to Newton's third law of motion, which states that for every action there is an equal and opposite reaction. The key things here are that forces must act in pairs and you get back what you give. In order to get more you need to give more. When you give you receive. For every force that one object experiences, there is another object that is subject to a force of equal strength that is in exactly the opposite direction.

How then do we get *more* quantitatively when this cornerstone in a universal principle of physics states that *exactly* what you put out you get back? It is because when this principle is applied to the interaction between human beings, there is a qualitative and intrinsic value that emerges from the action. We are conscious beings that process information and energy. It's about what it means to you. Think about a time when someone has fallen down and you literally "pick them back up." We have all performed that act at some point in our lives. But do we really think about it after doing it and what it meant to us? Most of the time we don't. It's almost a knee-jerk reaction to pick someone up if they have fallen down and then both parties go on their merry way. There is a lot more to it than that.

There are two people involved: there is a force that pushed the person down, and then we were the equal and opposite force that pulled them back up. That's the basic Newtonian law that we discussed. However, by delving deeper there is much more to it and many more forces involved. There is the force that propelled you to outstretch your hand and pick up the person in the first place. There is the force that created the feeling that you got when you picked up that person and he or she smiled at you and said "Thank you so much." There is the force that enabled someone to get back on their feet and perhaps get to their next job interview or pick up their children on time, and even perhaps spark a meaningful exchange between the two of you that resulted in a lucrative business transaction.

There is a reason why people use the phrase "it got me back on my feet" or "they helped me get back on my feet." Of course, people do not usually mean this phrase to be taken literally. It means something to them (the receiver) when someone helped them out as it enabled them to take the next step instead of being stagnant—or worse—digressing. It could be a game changer in someone's life. It also means something to you (the giver) as you quantitatively and qualitatively received something in return that brought you happiness.

So, the next time you are in a meeting and you want to offer up a revolutionary or innovative idea, but are afraid that you won't get credit for it or someone might take your idea—do it. You will see that many more, not less, opportunities come your way. The next time you can mentor someone by giving them some of your time and guidance—do it. You will set that person on a new path of abundance and also open a new one for yourself.

Giving also creates abundance in your life because it operates on the premise of creating space. In order for abundance and prosperity to come into your life it literally needs the space to do it. That is why it is said that to get more of anything, give more of it. When you give, you create the space for more of the same thing that you give to come back to you. I would add that not only more of what you give comes back to you, but also many other meaningful things come as an added bonus. I am sure you have noticed that a hole in the ground does not remain an empty hole for long. Sometimes it can provide a home for an animal and it is filled. It can grow weeds or be filled with water from the sky. It will never ever stay empty.

***Giving also creates abundance in your life because it operates on the premise of creating space. In order for abundance and prosperity to come into your life it literally needs the space to do it.***

Similarly, in a group brainstorming session, everyone is "giving" their ideas freely, and it allows the space for creativity to come rushing in. Some of the best ideas come from these settings where there is an exchange of information, and energy and space is created for that exchange, and that space is filled with innovation. This even holds true when you are working by yourself on something. I have had a feeling of being stuck or had a mental block, and I walked away (literally and mentally) from the situation, and seemingly out of nowhere a great idea came to me. By walking away, I created space for that idea. Sitting in my chair and beating my head against my laptop or pounding my fist on my desk only resulted in a headache and bruised fist. Not to mention wasted time. There was no space for the idea to come in.

Creating space for something to come in has another key component to it for human beings. This is where the word "freely" comes in when you read the trait titled "Give freely." Freely means that you get out of your own way. Freely means that you let go of your own inhibitions, prior assumptions, and ego to allow the space for the universe to let something in. This is very important. The person that told me to walk away from the project I was working on didn't impart me with a necessary detail, or if they did I didn't hear it. Walking away from my project only physically, but continuing to think about it, did not create any space. It was only when I truly let it go "freely" and gave it up for awhile that the space was created.

> ***You must give* freely *to create space. That means you have to let go of the expectation of receiving something, or that is all you will be left with—literally. The expectation will fill the space instead of the abundance and joy you were looking for.***

This concept of "giving freely" also applies when you give anything to others. Many times we give something with the expectation of receiving something in return, and we wait and wait and wonder why we didn't get what we gave. Remember, you must give freely to create space. That means you have to let go of the expectation of receiving something, or that is all you will be left with—literally. The expectation will fill the space instead of the abundance and joy you were looking for. There is no space for them to come in. Give without expecting anything in return. This is what giving freely means. Women do this naturally. We must go back to our true nature and realize that the real success or real gift comes back to us through giving freely.

## Cultivating the Art of Giving Freely and Expressing Gratitude

Be grateful. Feel and express gratitude—not because you have to *say* "thank you" as we are taught, but rather to *feel* "thank you" in your heart. Every day is truly a gift, as it is another opportunity to be the change and be happy. It is another day to breathe in the fresh air of life in our lungs that enables us to achieve our deepest desires on a spiritual, emotional, and even material level. Gratitude is another thing that cannot just be done as an action. It has to be felt within you in order to give it the energy that it needs to bring more of what you are grateful for in your life.

***Gratitude is another thing that cannot just be done as an action. It has to be felt within you in order to give it the energy that it needs to bring more of what you are grateful for in your life.***

People who only say "thank you" and don't really mean it are simply polite people, and that too is only on the surface. That's nice to be, but is that all you want to be? People that feel gratitude are appreciative of what they have, and by feeling this beautiful sentiment they take the energy away from the other places it could go—toward feelings of jealousy, envy, bitterness, anger, and resentment. No one wants more of those things in their lives. Again, abundance goes to where there is space. Feelings of gratitude are expansive in nature, and feelings of jealousy and bitterness are constrictive. One creates space, and the other does not.

### Yoga Pose: Offering or Honor *(Anjali Mudra)*

One great way to cultivate the practice of gratitude daily is to sit down and place your hands together in Anjali Mudra (pronounced, AHN-jah-lee MOO-dra). Anjali means "offering or honor" and Mudra means "seal." By placing your hands together at your heart center you are offering your deepest gratitude to the universe and sealing it with your intention of that particular moment. You are honoring yourself as well as all sentient beings, for we are all one.

- Sit comfortably on a chair or on the floor. This can be at home or in your office. As in meditation, it does not matter where you are or how long you do it; consistency is what is key. Close your eyes. Take a few breaths.
- Place your hands together at the level of your heart, and gently rest the knuckles of your thumbs against your sternum. It is nice to keep a little bit of space between the palms to allow the energy of gratitude to flow through from your heart to the universe and to all sentient beings.
- Bringing your palms together connects both the left and right hemispheres of your brain, representing unification of all that we are and promoting balance within. This mudra stimulates the pressure points in the palms and fingers, connecting the mind and body and infusing it with positive energy and sending it throughout our being to promote healing.

- This pose also soothes your mind and reduces mental anxiety as well.
- Notice the subtle shift in your mind, body, and spirit after you practice this simple but powerful pose.

***Offering or Honor Pose***
(Anjali Mudra)

I practice this pose daily at the beginning and end of my meditation practice, and it allows me to go within myself for a few moments and express my deepest gratitude for all the blessings that I have in my life—regardless of the forms that they come in. A life lesson that may not be pleasant is also a blessing as it creates the space for something wonderful to come in. A person that you work with or work for who is not the most pleasant person is a blessing since this person allows you to appreciate the people in your life that are a joy to be around.

Everything that happens to you in your life is happening for you. The biggest gifts often come disguised as challenges. They are opportunities to manifest your deepest intentions. Be grateful for what comes your way and create the space by giving feely to others and expressing gratitude daily for abundance to come rushing in.

***Everything that happens* to *you in your life is happening* for you.**

# SHOW GOOD WILL TO ALL

*Be fearless and pure;*
*never waver in your determination or*
*your dedication to the spiritual life.*
*Give freely. Be self-controlled,*
*sincere, truthful, loving,*
*and full of the desire to serve.*

*Realize the truth of the scriptures;*
*learn to be detached and to*
*take joy in renunciation.*
*Do not get angry or*
*harm any living creature,*
*but be compassionate and gentle;*
*show good will to all.*

*Cultivate vigor, patience, will purity;*
*avoid malice and pride.*
*Then, Arjuna, you will achieve*
*your divine destiny.*

—Bhagavad Gita

## Trait 7

# CONNECT WITH OTHERS AUTHENTICALLY

"I loved meeting her and talking with her ... she is so *authentic*." "He seemed so *authentic* in our negotiations that I left feeling like we both won." These are examples of some statements that we have either said about an interaction or heard someone say about an interaction or connection. The word "authentic" is italicized because when people choose to use that word they emphasize it and sometimes even put their hand on their heart when using it. Have you noticed that? Why is that?

Authenticity is one's true state of being—your Soul's Mirror. It is the state of being when you peel back all the layers of the onion of your self and you are left at the core. Your true self. Your authentic self. Your self that is devoid of masks and costumes that you wear throughout the day to play the role that you think you should be playing. This is your true state that some people only get glimpses of because they refuse to remove the mask.

***Authenticity is one's true state of being—your Soul's Mirror. It is the state of being when you peel back all the layers of the onion of your self and you are left at the core.***

You get glimpses of your authentic self when you are perhaps alone at night about to go to bed or alone in the shower. Or, perhaps this happens after meditation when you have just connected with your soul, because when you meditate there is no room for anyone else, as you are virtually naked and ethereal for all intents and purposes. The authentic person does not get glimpses of him/her self. He or she chooses to live and breathe in that state of being and that state of being is extremely magnetic.

There are three key traits to an authentic person. An authentic person is a person who has a very strong sense of self, is engaging, and actively listens when communicating with someone. People are attracted to this type of person and naturally gravitate towards this person. This is something that we want to cultivate within ourselves. We all have it within us to do so, but it takes real practice and willingness to shed your prior beliefs of yourself.

- Having a strong sense of self means that these people accept themselves for who they are and are very aware of who that person is. They accept both their positive and negative traits equally, and they always try to be the best version of themselves that they can be. When they look in the mirror they smile not only with their mouths, but with their eyes, which are the windows to their soul.
- A person that is engaging asks questions in a conversation of the other person or people, rather than it being all me, me, me. When you are engaging you are funny and not boring to whom you are speaking with, and you are able to have meaningful conversations with those outside your immediate social circle.
- A person who actively listens is truly present for the conversation being held. This is honestly the key to the authentic person. These persons have such a strong sense of self that they have no need to let their eyes wander around the room once the first thirty seconds of a conversation has passed, and they realize there is nothing in

it for them, or it has nothing to do with them. They are not looking down at their cell phone or watching television while they are having a conversation. They are nowhere else but right in front of you—physically, mentally, and spiritually. They are actively engaged with you and are actively listening to what is transpiring in the conversation. Active listening is also key because when you are not present for an exchange the other person can feel it and it changes the entire dynamic of the conversation. The conversation that could have been productive and meaningful turns into one that is transactional and really hollow.

## Cultivating the Art of Relating to Others Authentically

Connecting with others is vital to the human experience. When we connect with others we feel as though we are a part of something and all of our senses are stimulated. The experience becomes much more pleasurable when we connect with others as opposed to isolating ourselves and chalking it up to "being introverted." You must be able to connect with others in order to be successful in anything that you do. It is through connecting with others that deals are done, projects are completed, and new relationships are forged. This is called Networking. Networking is a term that has been coined to describe the art of connecting with others. However, this is something that is truly an art and does not come very easily to some people.

How do you connect with others if you are otherwise not inclined to do so or have challenges about connecting with others? This is something that I have run across countless times in my interactions. A lot of people label themselves as shy or introverted and wear that label as nametag when they meet others. It's not "Amy Parker" or "Lisa Smith" that is on the label, it's "Shy" or "Introverted" and this is how they walk into a room. The tone is set right then and there. These people hide behind those labels because they have not taken the time to get to know themselves, let alone accept themselves. It is easier. But this is nothing more than an excuse to not have to show others their authentic selves. Let's change that right here and now. Here are some great tips on how to connect with others that are virtual strangers and also people that you have met or connected with before, but not authentically:

- **Make eye contact and smile.** This is a huge icebreaker. When you do that, often the other person will shake your hand and greet you. Or, it will at least spark an initial connection for the other person to receive you by saying, "Hi, my name is . . ." One very small thing that women do more than men when dealing with people is that we smile more. This is very powerful. Even smiling on the phone when you speak or see someone produces an equal and opposite reaction and changes the tone of any meeting or interaction. Women tend to embrace when they meet. This is very welcoming and changes the tone of things. Even their handshake is a type of embrace as it is done with very warm and welcoming eye contact. A woman can make a very formidable opponent without anyone even knowing it because of these subtle characteristics.

- **Be engaging** by asking them how they are enjoying the event or asking them what brought them to the event in the first place. Avoid starting off the conversation with the standard, "So what do you do?" or "Where do you work?" Those are not engaging questions. Those questions have very direct answers, and they don't foster an authentic engagement. The authentic connection is one that is completely separate from what the person does for a living. It is about finding about more about who the person is and what interests them. Then, from here you can share what brought you to the event, etc. It becomes a very fluid exchange.

- **Connect them with someone else** who can benefit them or their interests. Generally speaking, women are better connectors than men. This is because when women network, they try to see how they can help the people they meet and then try to put other women together with like-minded goals. It is very collaborative in nature. When men network they try to help one another through doing each other favors, but for the majority, it stops at that one interaction. It does not go to the different degrees of connection that women do.

Women tend to make the environment and mood in the room less threatening and more inviting and relaxed. The mood becomes less adversarial and more corroborative. It rarely feels like you are doing business when in a room full of women, even when, very much to the contrary, many big deals are taking place. Of course, there are exceptions to the rule for both women and men. There are some women who are more adversarial and some men that are great collaborators and connectors beyond the first interaction.

## EFT (Emotional Freedom Technique)

I have found that a great way to cultivate the authentic connection with others is to go within and do a retune on ourselves and our entire nervous system. Until you deal with any underlying anxieties or fears you will inevitably project them onto your encounters with others. I have saved this technique of connecting well with others for the last chapter for a reason. You can also use this technique when you are dealing with an issue in the moment. The reason I chose to put it in the cultivation phase of the book rather than in the acute phase is that you want to get yourself to a place where you are in maintenance mode, so to speak.

If you keep doing the routine maintenance on your vehicle in a timely manner you will have less breakdowns and probably be able to catch an issue before it becomes into a mountain of a problem. Although this is unconventional with this technique as it is used mostly when there is an acute issue, I have found it to be quite effective as a maintenance tool as well.

The technique I have used over the past several years that does just this is called EFT (Emotional Freedom Technique™). Some people fondly call it "tapping." There are many books written on this fascinating and effective technique, and I encourage you to read them. However, I wanted to share some steps that I use to recalibrate, and I have noticed a difference in my outlook, mood, and overall health either immediately or within a few days after I do these.

The beauty of this technique is that you can do this anywhere and you do not need anyone to do it for you or with you. It takes only a few minutes to learn and each round takes about thirty seconds. You will do one to three rounds depending on how you are feeling at the time. A minute and a half at the most makes a significant impact in my emotional and physical well being . . . I'll take it! There are fabulous teachers all over the world, but in the event you choose not to make the time or have the inclination to join in with others, you can do this yourself.

This technique combines a tapping technique with positive affirmations. It is a type of psychological acupressure that really helps to optimize your emotional and, in turn, physical health. It is widely believed that physical issues often have emotional roots. Clearing those energy disruptions that cause the emotional imbalances can therefore also benefit your physical body as well. The combination of tapping along the energy meridians with vocalizing positive affirmations essentially stimulates the energy pathways and helps to balance any energy disruptions that may be occurring.

The EFT process has three main steps:

1. **Identifying an issue and assigning an intensity number to it**

   » This could be a negative event that happened today or recently or something that has bothered you for sometime.

   » You must be specific about the problem or event. You want to focus on the aspect that brings the most negative emotional and physical feeling to you.

   » For example: instead of focusing on a "general bad day at work," you will be ***specific*** and say, "when my boss, Diane, undermined me in the meeting by dismissing my idea without even hearing it through."

   » Assign a number to this feeling between zero and ten. Chances are it will be a ten when you start. This is key so that you can compare how you feel on the same scale after you complete the first round.

2. **Creating a Set-Up Statement**

   » This is a two-part statement that includes the specific issue that you have identified and a statement of self-acceptance.

   » It will be constructed like this: "Even though ________ ________________________________, I deeply and completely love and accept myself.

   » For the example we used about your boss undermining you, it would go something like this: "Even though my boss, Diane, undermined me in the meeting and made me feel insignificant, I completely and deeply love and accept myself."

   » You must create a mind and body connection with this. So, while saying the statement three times you will be tapping on the SETUP point, which is also called the Karate Chop point that is on the fleshy side of either hand. (see the picture of the lady below with the label "side of hand.")

» After saying this statement three times, all the while tapping on the SETUP point, you are ready to begin tapping!

3. **Following the Tapping Sequence**

» Below, please find a visual of the points on your body that you will be "tapping" with your index and middle fingers around five times. There is no need to count the taps, since anywhere between three to seven times is sufficient. Some people choose to use both hands as each point has its opposite point on the other side of your face and body. I was taught with one hand and it has been quite effective for me. They do not need to be done in the following sequence, but you will notice it's easier as each point is below the one before it. Remove your watch, bracelets, and glasses prior to starting.

» Side of hand (karate chop point-saying **set up statement** three times while tapping on this point).

Saying **Reminder Statements** while tapping these points:

- Top of Head
- Eyebrow
- Side of Eye
- Under Eye
- Under Nose
- Chin
- Collarbone (use three or four fingers to tap here so you don't miss the spot)
- Under Arm (use your palm here so you don't miss the spot)
- Wrist

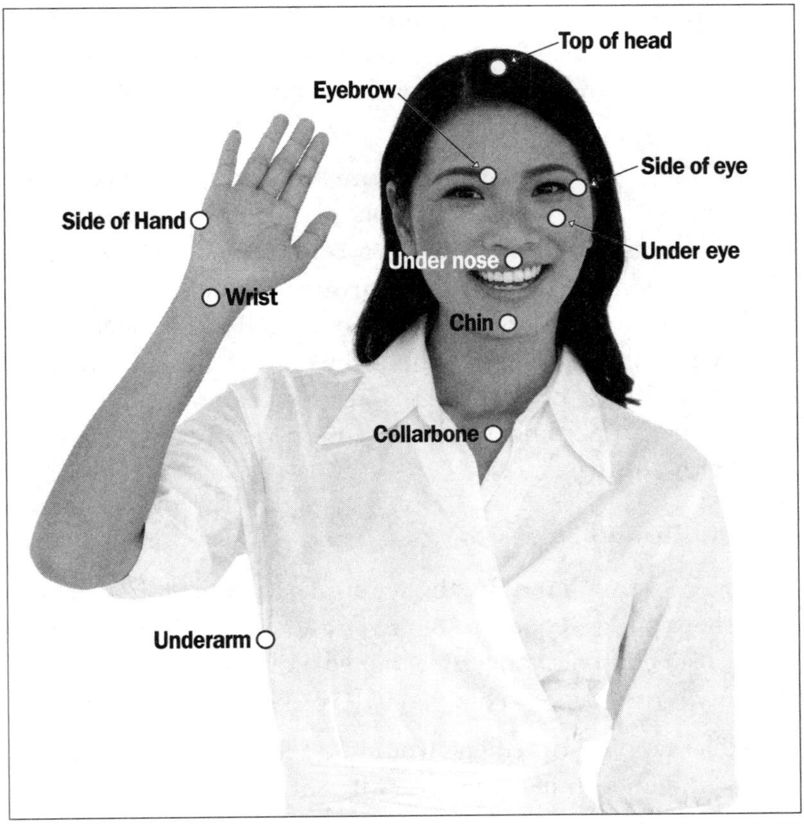


***EFT***
(Emotional Freedom Technique)

## *EFT tapping steps and statements instruction cheat sheet*

### First Round

- Begin by closing your eyes and taking a deep breath to center yourself.
- Repeat the Set Up phrase three times while tapping the karate chop point on your hand.
- Repeat a shortened Reminder phrase of the one you created as you tap each spot. **This is key**. For example, while tapping the rest of the points after the set up point you would

repeat the shortened reminder phrase of "feeling undermined and insignificant." Here you are getting to the bones of the feeling with a shortened statement for the tapping points.

» After you go through the entire sequence once, take a deep breath and observe how you are feeling at the moment. Are you still a ten? Did you go higher? Has it gone down to a seven? If it is anything greater than a two, repeat the sequence again until you get to around a two or less. This will probably be a few rounds. I like to do three rounds with most things: one to face the negative emotion, one to clear it out of my mind and body, and the final one to replace it with positive emotions.

**Second Round**

» Here you will modify the set up statement before you begin the tapping sequence to: "Even though I *still* have some of this feeling of being undermined and made insignificant by my boss, Diane, I completely love and accept myself."

» The tapping statement would be "The *remaining* feeling of being undermined and insignificant."

**Clearance Round and bringing in positivity**

» Here you have noticed a significant drop in intensity and are ready to clear the issue out of your mind and body.

» Once I am down to a two or less (preferably a zero), which will be around the third round, I do the final sequence and end with taking a deep breath and saying "I am breathing in love, light, and peace and exhaling any feelings of insignificance and feeling undermined by Diane."

» This last part is something I have chosen to add on as it helps me and is what I was taught. It is not part of the typical EFT practice. It seems to truly infuse my being with positive energy and the negative emotion is expelled from my body.

As with any technique, if you are feeling that it is not working for you or you are dealing with something particularly traumatic, please consult a licensed EFT Therapist or a doctor. This technique is something I wanted to share as I have found it to work for me and for millions of others. Happy Tapping!

Connecting with others authentically is the cornerstone to a successful, healthy, and happy journey through life. Without this you will not only hinder your success; you will be missing out on such a joyful, fulfilling experience.

# THE MORE SHALL WE LOVE

*We have to bear in mind that*
*we are all debtors to the world,*
*and that the world does not owe us anything.*
*It is a great privilege for all of us to be*
*allowed to do anything for the world.*
*In helping the world we truly help ourselves.*
*This world will always continue to be*

*a mixture of good and evil.*
*Our duty is to help*
*and sympathize with the weak,*
*and to love even the wrongdoer.*

*It is important to always keep in mind*
*that the world is for us a grand moral gymnasium,*
*wherein we are all blessed to be able to*
*take exercise in order to become*
*stronger and stronger spiritually.*

*The result of this exercise is that*
*the more selfless we become,*
*the more we shall love,*
*and the better will be our work.*

—SWAMI VIVEKANANDA

# AFTERWORD

I invite you to use this book as a guide and carry it around with you. After reading it end-to-end, I hope you will feel free to use it as you need in your daily journey through life. You can return to the 7 tools presented in part two to help cope with stressful situations and emotional issues that arise during the day, or find a resolution for the negative feelings from the long-standing problems described in these chapters that resonate with you.

Part three can be used at any time to practice a daily cultivation of the OM Factor. A great way to practice is to focus on one trait every day and to read that chapter right before you do your meditation and the yoga pose to cultivate that trait.

The poems from various sacred works throughout the book, that are intended to increase our daily awareness of our spiritual connection to the divine within ourselves and others, are also a wonderful way to start your day, end your day, or seal in your practice with reflection.

I wish you peace, love, light, and manifestation of your deepest desires. You now have the tools now to cultivate your own OM FACTOR and bring it to every aspect of your life and others.

# ACKNOWLEDGMENTS

My deepest debt of gratitude to my mother, Asha Sethi. Through your daily selfless sacrifices, you are the reason that I have the freedom to dream and make my life which feels like a dream a reality.

*Many thanks to:*

Amar, for the priceless gift of time. You gave me the time, space, and support to put pen to paper and write what came to me from the universe.

Yuvraj, you are my soul's compass. Thank you for believing in me and for your unwavering faith in *The OM Factor*. Thank you for continuing to push me to places within myself where there are no limits. This book would have not been possible without you.

Aria, you are my heart, and I truly hope I can come back and be you in my next lifetime. Your strong sense of self is unmatched and I am in awe of how you navigate through life. You are the reason I strive to be the best mother I can be.

Manisha, for always being my biggest fan and wind beneath my wings. You are always there by my side as an eternal optimist. Thank you as well for your professional advice throughout this process that was so valuable to me.

Seema, for being the mirror of the state of my soul. Thank you for your love, loyalty, and above all your authenticity.

Gagan, for being my friend and colleague. I have been blessed to have two very distinct and real relationships with you. Our conversations have inspired me and sharing space with you is so special.

Sanjay, for your broad shoulders that I have leaned on a number of times when I really needed it.

Anu, immortal, eternal, and forever a part of my soul.

Papa, for teaching me about the awakening of Kundalini and its sacred power. Thank you for also teaching me that things are not as serious as they can sometimes seem.

Binu, for the comfort of sharing silence and being able to communicate without words.

Kavita, for showing me the true meaning of family-first, and being a great role model for me.

Pawan, for living your life by your own rules and own inner guidance. I admire that so much.

Rachna, my soul sister. So nice to be on this path with you.

Manu, for always being there for me. Day or night, whenever I reached out no matter where you were in the world at the time.

Kunal, for "getting me" and our long, unfiltered talks.

Diya, for your belief in my writing and my path. I know when you put pen to paper your words and ideas will influence millions and Be The Change. I look forward to seeing this.

Adrienne, for being my sounding board and pulse throughout the entire journey of this labor of love. Our soul connection is one that I cherish so deeply.

Rebecca, for enabling me to continue pursuing my entrepreneurial dreams and being such an amazingly loving and positive influence on my children daily.

Natalia, for your creativity and being my cheerleader throughout this entire process. Thank you for your genuine interest in this book and its message.

Deepak, thank you for being you in this lifetime. You have taught me so much and most importantly how to tap into my inner wisdom through being in the gap. I am so grateful to you.

Jean, for teaching me how to access my inner archetypes through self-discovery and introspection to bring out the Wizard in me. You have been so generous with your time and, most importantly, your heart, in providing me valuable and timely guidance.

Bill Gladstone, my agent, for sage advice whenever I needed it throughout this process. Thank you for believing in me, my message, and *The OM Factor*.

Kenzi and Kenichi, thank you for your belief in this book and desire to get it out into the universe.

Nancy, thank you for your laser-like focus, attention to detail, and giving this book attention and care.

Houri, for your guidance and love from the time my father left this earth to now.

Anne, for always keeping me in prayer and sending me love and light every time you sit in silence.

My spiritual advising team: Carolyn, Tina, Tejpal, Maggie, Sari, Brent, Tim and Pam: for being conduits of timely, accurate, and loving advice from the cosmos to me.

Michael Tompkins, for being my trusted advisor and champion of *The OM Factor*. Thank you for going above and beyond to help this book succeed and reach so many people.

Edie Fraser, for your friendship and mentorship. Thank you for always looking out for my best interests and aligning me with things that have helped my career and personal development greatly.

Diana Davis Spencer, for your selfless desire to help me and connecting me with the right people to get this book and its message out into the universe.

# ILLUSTRATION AND PHOTOGRAPH CREDITS

| | |
|---|---|
| page 18 | Image source: Shutterstock Photo, copyright Bolarkina Marina |
| page 76 | Photo: © i love images, Fotolia.com<br>Drawing of hands © 2014 Joyce Mihran Turley |
| page 127 | Illustration © 2014 Joyce Mihran Turley |
| page 138 | Copyright Nanka Shutterstock.com |
| page 139 | Copyright Nanka, Shutterstock.com |
| page 140 | Copyright iStock.com/NadyaPhoto |
| page 152 | Copyright Zdenka Darula Shutterstock.com |
| page 165 | Copyright Lucky Business, Shuttercock.com |
| page 175 | Copyright Zdenka Darula, Shutterstock.com |
| page 185 | Copyright Lucky Business, Shutterstock.com |
| page 197 | Copyright WavebreakmediaMicro, Fotolia.com |

# ABOUT THE AUTHOR

Alka Dhillon is the founder and Chief Executive Officer of Technalink, Inc., one of the leading technology companies in the Washington Metropolitan area. Technalink has provided information technology (IT) services and management consulting solutions to both government and commercial clients for fifteen years. Ms. Dhillon has over nineteen years' experience in the information technology and management consulting industry.

In addition to her responsibilities as CEO of Technalink, Ms. Dhillon uses her passion for technology as platform to give back. She is committed to empowering youth to explore entrepreneurship and careers in science and technology. Ms. Dhillon is passionate about science, technology, engineering, and math (STEM) and is a keynote speaker to the Girls in Technolgy organization (GIT) on the subject of entrepreneurism to inspire more girls to pursue STEM related careers. Ms. Dhillon is actively involved in the Network for Teaching Entrepreneurship (NFTE) and serves as a board member.

Ms. Dhillon has been honored with numerous awards, not only for her professional achievements, but also for her commitment to serving her community. Her accolades include receiving the 2012 BRAVA! Women Business Achievement Award presented by SmartCEO, the Top 100 Women Leaders in STEM, the 2013 Locally Grown honor by Network for Teaching Entrepreneurship (NFTE) and the Abe Veneable Legacy Award for Lifetime Achievement presented by the U.S. Department of Commerce's Minority Business Agency (MBDA).

Ms. Dhillon holds B.A. degrees in economics and Spanish from the University of Virginia.

For more information about *The OM Factor*, visit www.alkadhillon.com. She also contributes to *The Huffington Post* and blogs at her website The Spiritual CEO, www.thespiritualceo.com.